Lorca's New York poetry

For Pat

Lorca's New York poetry

Social injustice, dark love, lost faith

Richard L. Predmore

Duke University Press   Durham, N.C.   1980

Much of the preparation of this book was
made possible by a grant from the John Simon
Guggenheim Memorial Foundation.

Quotations from Lorca's poetry are from
Federico García Lorca, *Obras Completas*,
copyright © Herederos de Federico García
Lorca 1954. Reprinted by permission of New
Directions, New York, Agents.

Contents

Preface

It has been nearly fifty years now since Federico García Lorca wrote the poems that constitute *Poeta en Nueva York*, and yet in some ways they read like a book written yesterday. Their themes of materialism, of dehumanization, of violence, of social and racial injustice could have been taken from today's headlines. Because they seem to speak so powerfully to and about the contemporary world, one could imagine them attracting more readers today than they did when first published in 1940. If they do not, it is partly because the difficulties of interpreting them reliably are so varied and arduous. Some of the difficulties are adventitious, some can be attributed to the nature of the poetry itself. It is necessary to mention these difficulties so that the reader may judge for himself whether and to what extent they may compromise the interpretations offered in this study.

The difficulties I have called adventitious proceed from the accidental imperfections of existing editions. There are textual problems of all kinds: bizarre punctuations, textual variants serious enough to affect the interpretations of certain verses, and, above all, doubts about the structural integrity of a text that remained unpublished until four years after the author's death.

To understand why there are doubts about the structural integrity of *Poeta en Nueva York*, it will be helpful to review briefly the strange and complicated history of the first two editions, which in 1940 appeared within two or three weeks of one another.[1] The front matter of the Mexican edition says about the original only that its editor, José Bergamín, received it directly from García Lorca (p. 8). Rolfe Humphries, translator of the Norton edition, does not say how he came into possession of the typescript he used, but he does say it was not always perfectly clear, that he sometimes felt obliged to try to establish the text, and that he was unable to locate three poems which, according to the typescript, the poet intended to include in the collection (p. 17). These three poems are: "Tu infancia en Menton," "Amantes asesinados por una perdiz," and "Crucifixión." Bergamín published only the first of these three poems. Humphries further says that he has included two poems lacking in the type-script: "Paisaje con dos tumbas y un perro asirio" and "Vals en las ramas." Both of these poems also appear in the Mexican edition. For reasons nowhere explained, the Norton edition places the poem called "La aurora" third in section 1 while the Mexican edition places it last in section 3. Later editions follow the Mexican edition.

From the above it does not seem venturesome to conclude that both editions were based on the same original, that the original was unclear in certain places, that some of the poems were present only as titles of poems intended for inclusion, that both the Spanish editor and the American translator took the liberty of adding two poems not mentioned in the typescript, and that the Spanish editor permitted himself to place "La aurora" out of the order presumably indicated in the typescript. Subsequent editions of *Poeta en Nueva York* contained in the *Obras completas* published by Aguilar retain the two poems not mentioned in the typescript and add "Crucifixión" and "Pequeño poema infinito," both of which the poet probably meant to be part of *Poeta en Nueva York*.[2] The prose piece "Amantes asesinados por una perdiz" has never been

1. The first to appear was *The Poet in New York and Other Poems of Federico García Lorca*, trans. Rolfe Humphries (New York: W. W. Norton & Co., 1940). The second was *Poeta en Nueva York* (México, D.F.: Editorial Séneca, 1940). Both carry substantially the same introduction by José Bergamín.

2. In August of 1935 Lorca wrote to his friend Miguel Benítez Inglott requesting the return of "Crucifixión," which he claims will be one of the best poems in *Poeta en Nueva York*. In a follow-up letter written in the same month, he repeats his request for the manu-script of "Crucifixión" and inquires about the manuscript of a poem called "Pequeño poema

published with the New York poems despite Humphries's statement that it is called for in the typescript.

There is evidence of several other specific titles that Lorca may have intended to form part of his New York book.[3] All of these poems are now available in recent editions of his complete works but not necessarily in an order determined by the author. Mention should be made of at least one other uncertainty about the book as it has come down to us. In a 1933 interview the poet applies to his manuscript the words "enormous" and "very long."[4] Where, one may wonder, are the poems that would justify calling the book enormous? Is it possible that in 1933 the poet conceived of his book on a much larger scale than he did when he was having the manuscript typed in the fall of 1935 to give for publication to his friend Bergamín? The book as we now have it in the Aguilar editions contains only sixty-two small pages and represents the same poems published by Bergamín plus "Crucifixión" and "Pequeño poema infinito."

I have far from exhausted the mysteries connected with the history of *Poeta en Nueva York*,[5] but I have presented enough to permit the reader to ponder this question: Is it rationally possible to attach any significance to the way *Poeta en Nueva York* is organized in the editions now regularly used? In other words, can one assume that a meaningful organization reflecting the author's expressive intentions is present in the book as we know it? Despite everything said in the preceding paragraphs, the answer is probably Yes. The first two editions and all subsequent ones present the book divided into the same ten sections, each with the same subtitle. Where could this structural uniformity originate but in the typescript given by Lorca to Bergamín? Within this frame-

---

infinito." Although he does not say it was for the New York collection, it seems reasonable to suppose it was, since the letters reveal that he was then preparing the manuscript for printing. See Lorca's *Obras completas* (Madrid: Aguilar, 1966), pp. 1671–72. All quotations from Lorca will be from this edition unless otherwise specified.

3. See Ben Belitt, "A Critical Chronology," in *Poet in New York* (New York: Grove Press, 1955), pp. 185–91.

4. See *Obra completas*, p. 1730. Marie Laffranque is persuaded that as much as half of the projected book may remain unpublished. As evidence she cites a statement by Méndez Domínguez in which he claims to have read some 250 pages of the New York poems and one by Lorca announcing 300 pages. See her *Les Idées Esthétiques de Federico García Lorca* (Paris: Centre de Recherches Hispaniques, 1967), p. 226.

5. A number of scholars are working to clear up the textual problems of *Poeta en Nueva York*. Eutimio Martín has written an article called "¿Existe una versión definitiva de *Poeta en Nueva York*?" *Insula* 310 (Sept. 1972): 1, 10. The fullest account of these problems is Daniel Eisenberg's *"Poeta en Nueva York": historia y problemas de un texto de Lorca* (Barcelona: Editorial Ariel, 1976).

work all of the dated poems occupy the same places in all editions even though the order followed is not chronological. Finally, the first two editions differ structurally only in two poems out of thirty-one: the different placing of "La aurora" and the addition in the Mexican edition of "Tu infancia en Menton." Surely it is plausible, then, to think that over 90 percent of *Poeta en Nueva York* in its present form reflects the organization that Lorca gave it in the fall of 1935.

The difficulties that I have said could be attributed to the nature of the poetry itself are the difficulties inherent in any highly personal symbolic system, especially one that is deliberately thorny. At the very end of his famous lecture, "Imagination, Inspiration, Evasion," Lorca said: "Poetry does not want initiates but lovers. It puts up brambles and broken glass so that the hands which seek it may wound themselves for love" (p. 91). The aim of the present study is to penetrate the brambles and the broken glass in order to explore and elucidate the poetic symbolism and thematic structure of *Poeta en Nueva York*. Before attempting that exploration directly, I found it useful to write three preliminary chapters: one to collect and interpret the ideas and attitudes about poetry that were in the poet's mind when he undertook his New York journey, one to determine in what measure the poetic language of the new book can be understood in the light of the ambiguous symbolism already developed in earlier works, and one to describe the book in some first approximation of its overall meaning.

Although *Poeta en Nueva York* is undeniably a major work by a major poet, it has not yet received the kind of critical attention it deserves. Several critics have offered some kind of overall interpretation of the work, but none has really taken the whole book into account or even succeeded in accounting for all the elements of any one poem. The reason for this general incompleteness is not hard to imagine: many passages in many poems are abstruse in the extreme. The most common way of handling these passages is to ignore them; another way is to advance conjecture without so labeling it. Far from me to claim that I have solved all the riddles of the New York poems, but I have tried to avoid the stratagems mentioned above. I have taken pains to let the reader know which of my readings of the poems I think are relatively complete and accurate and which remain problematical. I have sometimes resorted to the kind of conjectures that rest on long and intimate acquaintance with all of Lorca's poetry, but if they are conjectures that is the way I present them.

I am sure that some of my interpretations will strike readers of this study as fanciful or far-fetched. Had I found them a few years ago in someone else's book, I would have considered them improbable. Now I am confident that most of them are essentially sound. All I ask of the reader is that he suspend final judgment until he has judged all the pieces of the puzzle.

All verse quoted in this study is presented first in Lorca's Spanish and then in my English. In translating I have striven more for accuracy than for poetic effect. I have not thought it necessary to provide the original Spanish of prose quotations.

Whatever this study may contribute to a fuller understanding of the New York poems should also be a contribution to the understanding of all of Lorca's works, since I have used them all in developing my interpretation of *Poeta en Nueva York*.

Lorca's New York poetry

1

Psychic afflictions and poetic notions

"With Federico everything was inspiration, and his life, so beautifully in accord with his work, was the triumph of liberty, and between his life and his work there is a spiritual and physical interchange so constant, so passionate and fruitful, that it makes them eternally inseparable and indivisible. In this sense, as in many others, he reminds me of Lope."[1] Vicente Aleixandre wrote these words about a year after the death of his friend Federico García Lorca. Despite the well-known risks of assuming the kind of consonance between life and works attributed to his friend by Aleixandre, his words make a good starting point for this chapter. In it we will sample and relate what Lorca had to say about personal problems and about poetry in the two or three years immediately prior to his departure for New York.

Many critics have speculated about the reasons that prompted Lorca to travel to New York. One of the reasons suggested is that he wanted to escape the facile fame accorded him by the success of his *Romancero gitano*, a success

1. "Federico," by Vicente Aleixandre, in Federico García Lorca, *Obras completas*, p. 1830.

that seemed to characterize him as a regional poet with only one main theme: gypsyism. As a matter of fact, in a letter to Jorge Guillén he complains about this myth even before the publication of *Romancero gitano*.[2] Another reason that may have inclined him to go to New York is that his friend and mentor, Fernando de los Ríos, was making the trip and would help him get established there. But these are secondary considerations. Most critics assume that deeply felt personal problems aroused in him the desire to leave for a while the familiar haunts of Granada and Madrid. Angel del Río refers to "an emotional crisis in the life of the poet" and goes on to state that his "anguish was a real one, as were also the personal gloom and emotional preoccupations which he lived through during these months. The sources of this emotional crisis are obscure, at least for those who knew him superficially. They touch delicate fibers of his personality, problems which cannot be hastily appraised or dismissed, but which left a very real impact on the book; so only when they are taken into consideration can the work, or at least some parts of it, be understood in all its significance."[3] Juan Larrea, another of Lorca's friends, expresses his opinion more frankly: "When he wrote this book, Federico García Lorca was the victim of a painful inner crisis. Everything indicates that this crisis was in large part the result of a sexual anomaly. He is unable to adjust. He cannot live a satisfying life in a society that rejects as a dishonorable defect his congenital abnormality, neither depraved nor infamous."[4] In their allusions to intimate problems reflected in his book, these critics confirm Aleixandre's opinion about the constant interchange in Lorca between his life and his works, but perhaps it is unnecessary to appeal to the external facts of his biography to understand his poetry.

The emotional preoccupations that del Río mentions in relation to the poet's sojourn in New York were already painfully at work at least two years before he left for America. In a series of letters written in 1927 to his Catalan friend, Sebastian Gasch, he frequently refers to an emotional crisis. In one of the earlier letters of that year, he writes: "My spiritual state is not what you would

2. See *Obras completas*, p. 1614.

3. Introduction to Ben Belitt's translation of *Poeta en Nueva York*, p. xiv. Clemente Fusero suggests that Lorca's trip was determined by a "long sentimental storm." See his *García Lorca* (Milano: Dall 'Oglio, 1969), p. 273. In discussing "Poema doble del lago Edem" Marie Laffranque refers to Lorca's "intimate conflicts." See her *Les Idées Ethétiques*, p. 225. Jean-Louis Schonberg believes Lorca was upset by the cooling of his friendship with Salvador Dalí. See his *Federico García Lorca: El hombre, la obra* (Mexico: Compañía general de ediciones, 1959), p. 94.

4. See "Asesinado por el cielo," *España Peregrina* 1 (1940): 252.

call good. I am passing through a great sentimental crisis (that's right) from which I hope to emerge cured" (p. 1644). But the cure does not come as soon as expected. In later letters he refers to forbidding terrains, dark mirrors, and the abyss. Here is an example: "I never venture into terrains not proper to man, because I turn back at once and almost always destroy the product of my trip. . . . My state is ever joyful, and this dreaming of mine is not dangerous in me, because I have defenses; it is dangerous for him who lets himself be fascinated by the great dark mirrors that poetry and madness put at the bottom of their ravines. *I am and feel myself to be lead-footed in Art.* It is in the reality of my life, in love, in the daily encounter with others that I *fear* dreaming and the abyss. That is indeed terrible and fantastic" (p. 1656). We must not be misled by the joyfulness affirmed above: against deep troubles it was only a superficial defense.

In the poet's words just quoted, Lorca seems inclined to separate certain things experienced in his own life from what he is willing to include in his art. As we shall later see, in the end he determined not to exclude from the possibilities of art any part of his personal experience. The following quotation referring to his drawings represents an intermediate stage in his thinking: "Of course I find myself at this time with an almost physical sensibility which carries me to planes [of reality] where it is difficult to keep one's footing and where one almost flies over the abyss. It is enormously difficult for me to maintain a normal conversation with these people at the resort, because my eyes and my words are elsewhere. They are in the immense library that nobody has read, in a fresh breeze, a country where things dance with one foot" (pp. 1657–58). The probable significance of these references to strange and unknown regions of human experience will become clearer as the chapter progresses.[5] In the meantime it should be noted that the artist now says little about the dangers of letting his art lead him into those regions.

In 1928 expressions of unhappiness continue. A few excerpts from a letter to Jorge Zalamea reveal the state of his mind and spirit: "I have had a very bad time. Very bad. It is necessary to have the amount of gaiety God has given me not to succumb before the number of conflicts that have assaulted me recently. . . . Now I have a poetry of *opening one's veins*, a poetry

5. A number of other early twentieth-century artists wrote in terms very similar to Lorca's. Consider, for example, these words from W. Kandinsky's famous little book, *Concerning the Spiritual in Art* (1912): "The tortuous paths of the new world will lead through dark primeval forests and over bottomless chasms, toward icy peaks, with the same unfailing guide—the unchanging principal of internal necessity" (quoted from the English version published in New York by George Wittenborn, 1947, p. 72).

freed from reality and with an emotion in which is reflected all my love of things and my joking about things. Love of dying and mockery of dying. Love. My heart. That's the way it is. . . . One must be joyful, it is a duty to be joyful. I tell you so, who am passing through one of the saddest and most disagreeable moments of my life" (p. 1664). In a still later letter to Zalamea he claims to have overcome his painful state, but it is clear that he has not. Here is a significant fragment of the letter: "During these days I have resolved by will power one of the most painful states that I have had in my life. You can't imagine what it is to spend entire nights on the balcony seeing a nocturnal Granada *empty* for me and without the slightest consolation of any kind. And then . . . Trying constantly to keep your state from filtering into your poetry, because it would play on you the dirty trick of opening the purest part of you to the glances of those who must never see it" (p. 1666).

There are still more confessions like the ones already exhibited. I choose one more from some words published in *El Defensor de Granada* on 7 May 1929, a scant two months before Lorca landed in New York: "Now more than ever, I need the silence and spiritual density of Granada's air to sustain the duel to death that I sustain with my heart and with poetry. With my heart to free it from the impossible destructive passion and from the deceitful shadow of the world that spatters it with sterile sunshine; with poetry to construct, despite her defending herself like a virgin, the wide-awake and true poem where beauty and horror and the ineffable and the repugnant may live and collide in the midst of the most incandescent joy" (pp. 129–30).

From the quotations thus far adduced several things stand out: Lorca's emotional problems were prolonged and severe, they seem to have been born of some consuming passion, and they appear to have associated themselves in one way or another with his thinking about his art. Sometimes he shows himself disposed to defend his artistic creations from infiltrations of psychic experiences which in imitation of his diction we might call abyssal; sometimes he shows himself disposed to use those experiences to carry his art into regions not yet won for Spanish poetry. But if the nature of the emotional crises that troubled him in the two or more years preceding his sojourn in America turned his thoughts with increasing frequency and intensity to the poetic possibilities of strange, new modes of feeling and expression, such thoughts were really part of a life-long quest.

From the beginning of his poetic career, Lorca yearned, as most young poets do, to create a poetic world of his own. In a lecture about "deep song" delivered in February of 1922, he said of young Claude Debussy that he was involved "in that terrible struggle that all we young artists have to sustain, the struggle for something new, something unforeseen, the plunge (*buceo*) into the sea of thought in search of emotion still intact" (p. 43). Lorca not only joined that struggle for novelty but came to conceive of it in terms of mortal risk. In his celebrated lecture on the daemon (*duende*), he claimed that the daemon does not attend the poet unless "he sees the possibility of death," because "he likes to wrestle with the creator on the brink of the pit" (p. 117). These words are in keeping with the already quoted statement about his duel to the death with his heart and his poetry.[6]

If Lorca represented poetic creation as a hazardous undertaking, perhaps it was because he understood that his poetry was to be, at least in part, the exploration of dark and dangerous terrain. The vocabulary used to express that exploration is revealing. We have already noted the phrase "to plunge into the sea of thought." Another capital word is the nautical term "to sound" (*sondar*). In his first book of verse, there are at least two typical examples:

El presentimiento
es la sonda del alma
en el misterio.

Nariz del corazón,
que explora en la tiniebla
del tiempo.   (p. 213)

> Presentiment
> is the sounding lead
> of the soul in mystery.
>
> Nose of the heart,
> that explores in the
> dark of time.

6. Marcel Raymond in his *De Baudelaire au Surréalisme* (1933) also speaks of the dangerous conquest of the new poetry as understood by the surrealists: "The essence of the surrealist message consists in this call for the absolute freedom of the mind, in the affirmation that life and poetry are 'elsewhere,' and that they must be conquered dangerously . . ." (quoted by H. Read in *A Concise History of Modern Painting* (New York: Praeger, 1968), p. 145. Lorca denied, no doubt correctly, that he was a surrealist, but it is obvious that his New York poems show more than a little resemblance to the poetry of surrealism. Nevertheless, I believe Betty Jean Craige is correct in saying that despite the surrealistic images in *Poeta en Nueva York* it is not surrealist poetry. For the rationale of that judgment, see her *Lorca's Poet in New York* (Lexington: The University of Kentucky Press, 1977), pp. 45–46.

Bajo tu casta sombra, encina vieja,
quiero sondar la fuente de mi vida
y sacar de los fangos de mi sombra
las esmeraldas líricas.   (p. 279)[7]

> Under your chaste shade, old oak,
> I wish to sound the fountain of my life
> and take from my shadow's mire
> the lyrical emeralds.

In one of the poems of *Poeta en Nueva York* the author calls himself *"un pulso herido que sonda las cosas del otro lado"* ("a wounded pulse which probes things from the other side"), p. 499. He sensed that something of what he sought quivered in the obscure depths of his biological being.[8] That's why, he thought, one had to awaken the daemon "in the deepest abodes of the blood" (p. 111). He wanted to understand, wherever it might be found, "the truth of mistaken things" (p. 500). In the second poem quoted above, he proposed to extract lyric emeralds from the mire of his shadow. That digging in mud or mire (*cieno*) was a key notion is suggested by its repetition in another stanza of the same poem:

Echo mis redes sobre el agua turbia
y las saco vacías.
¡Más abajo del cieno tenebroso
están mis pedrerías!   (p. 279)

> I cast my nets upon the roily water
> and empty draw them forth.
> Down below the darkling mud
> are found my precious stones!

7. I have no reason to believe that Lorca knew the works of Carl Jung, but in the poet's writings there is much to remind the reader of the theories of that psychologist. Compare, for example, this quotation with the poems already quoted: "In the process of realizing and assimilating an unconscious content, the ego makes a 'descent,' from the conscious standpoint, into the depths, in order to raise up the 'treasure.'" See Erich Neumann, *The Origins and History of Consciousness*, foreword C. G. Jung, trans. R. F. C. Hull (Princeton, N.J.: Princeton University Press, 1970), p. 343.

8. The line of inquiry we are following brings to mind a suggestive characterization of Lorca by Salvador Dalí: "On the other hand, the personality of Federico García Lorca produced an immense impression on me. The poetic phenomenon in its entirety and 'in the raw' presented itself before me suddenly in flesh and bone, confused, blood-red, viscous and sublime, quivering with a thousand fires of darkness and of subterranean biology, like all matter endowed with the originality of its own form." See Dalí's *The Secret Life of Salvador Dalí* (New York: Dial Press, 1942), p. 176.

Still further on in the poem the poet speaks of taking false gems from the mud of sleeping passions.

It is time to ask what is the meaning of the special vocabulary I have been exhibiting. What does it mean to plunge, to take soundings, to delve in shadow, darkness, mud, and mire for things of beauty and value? The answer seems to be that the poet would pursue his poetic quest into the darkest depths of his psychic and biological being.

The new beauty that Lorca sought and attained was due in part to the nature of the experiences he wanted to express and in part to the novelty of the art he practiced. It will take several chapters to analyze that art. In the meantime preliminary orientation may be found in some of the critical remarks the poet scattered throughout his works. The enthusiasm with which he discoursed on the poetic language of Góngora allows one to suspect that part of what he said about Góngora's art may be applicable to his own.[9] Consider this statement: "Naturally, Góngora does not create his images after Nature herself but carries the object, thing or act to the camera obscura of his brain whence they emerge transformed to make the great leap onto the other world with which they are fused" (p. 73). Although Lorca's poetry is very different from Góngora's, the quoted words well describe the extraordinary metamorphoses that things undergo in the camera obscura of his brain.

Two texts dating from the year before his trip to America throw some light on Lorca's poetic orientation. One of the texts is his lecture on imagination, inspiration, and evasion. In it he said that most recent generations of poets aspired "to free poetry not only from anecdote but also from the riddle of the image and from the planes of reality. . . ." (pp. 88–89); then he spoke of an "evasion of reality by the path of dreams, by the path of the subconscious, by the path dictated by an utterly unusual fact that is the gift of inspiration" (p. 89). The other text is a letter to his friend Sebastian Gasch. It deals with two prose poems just sent to Gasch. Lorca comments: "They correspond to my new spiritualist manner, pure, fleshless emotion, unbound from logical control, but take heed: with a tremendous poetic logic. It is not surrealism, take heed: the clearest consciousness illuminates them" (p. 1654).

With the quotations brought together in this chapter, we can sum up that part of Lorca's feeling and thinking most likely to help us understand the poems he was to write about his American experience. It is important to

9. Marie Laffranque believes that these early ideas about Góngora were soon superseded, and she may be right. See her Les Idées Esthétiques, p. 115. Nevertheless, some of what he said in his lecture helps to understand his own poetics.

remember that he was still in the throes of an emotional crisis which sometimes seemed to associate itself in his mind with the creation of a new poetry.
He conceived of poetic creation as a perilous struggle for the new, the unusual,
the unforeseen.[10] To create a new poetry, he thought, the writer must venture
into dangerous realms, descend to the most turbid regions of biological being,
be willing to take soundings among things from the other side, that is, from
beyond reason, consciousness, and social convention. Freed from anecdotes
and the guessing game of images, his poetry would express pure emotion, cut
loose from logical bindings, but not for that reason surrealistic, because it
would have a consciously created poetic logic.

Human curiosity and literary tradition being what they are, it is unlikely
that readers can approach the strange and disturbing beauty of *Poeta en Nueva
York* without trying to solve the riddle of the images or seeking to discover
the anecdote, however shadowy, that may lurk in the background of a poem.
But apparent failure to solve these puzzles will not be total failure if we heed
the poet's hints and succeed in understanding the structured meaning of the
emotions expressed in the New York poems.[11]

10. This attitude toward artistic creation is widespread in modern times. Here is a
relevant reminder by Renato Poggioli: "The ancients and the classical writers tended to give
a lucid and pitiless criticism of the new, but the moderns almost always yield to the tempta-
tion to seek, without truce or peace, the unknown zones of art and culture. To discover
unheard-of zones, the modern spirit is disposed to scale heaven and violate hell, to descend,
according to Baudelaire's verse, 'Au fond de l'inconnu pour trouver du nouveau'" (*The
Theory of the Avant-Garde* [New York: Harper & Row, 1971], p. 225).

11. Writing of archetypal imagery in one phase of Picasso's painting, Herbert Read has
this to say: "To reveal the significance of the symbols is not a useful activity: they remain
most potent in their secret integrity" (*A Concise History of Modern Painting*, p. 160). If this
is true, it is probably truer of painting than of poetry. Still, some of the obscure symbols of
Lorca's most difficult poems do impress the reader with their mysterious power.

2

The rhetoric of ambiguity

The purpose of this chapter is to study some aspects of the figurative language that Lorca used so effectively to create his highly original poetic world. The nature of this world is quite unlike the popular public image of Lorca prevalent in his own day. So many of his friends and critics have testified to his incomparable gaiety in their midst that it is possible to forget, or at least to minimize, the dark and introspective side of his nature.[1] A careful reading of his poems reveals a man who often felt himself caught in the tormenting tensions of opposing forces, whether within his own personality or within the inescapable

Some of the material in this chapter was published in Spanish in an essay called "Simbolismo ambiguo en la poesía de García Lorca, *Papeles de Son Armadans* 189 (1971): 229–40.

1. Compare these words by the poet's brother Francisco: "How many times, on the great stage of the world, his life was a performance. . . . It included, sometimes, the exorcising of the shadow which lay behind his gaze even during the contagious moments of his laughter." See *Three Tragedies of Federico García Lorca* (New York: New Directions, 1947), pp. 6–7.

constraints of a human destiny conceived as involving the conflict of passing love and abiding death unconsoled by the possibility of divine grace. Unable to resolve these tensions, he gave powerful expression in his poetry to what it felt like to experience them.

The quickest way to gain some sense of the fields of conflicting forces that dominate Lorca's poetic world is to observe how frequently in *Poeta en Nueva York* he combines words that would ordinarily be at each other's throats. Here is a sample of the combinations I have in mind: *"la feria de ceniza"* ("the fair of ashes"), p. 472; *"meriendan muerte los borrachos"* ("the drunks picnic on death"), p. 474; *"clínica y selva de la anatomía"* ("clinic and jungle of anatomy"), p. 476; *"la tierna intimidad de los volcanes"* ("the tender intimacy of the volcanoes"), p. 495; *"una pequeña quemadura infinita"* ("a little infinite burn"), p. 495; *"las fiebres pequeñas heladas"* ("the small frozen fevers"), p. 501; *"flores de terror"* ("flowers of terror"), p. 502; *"las tres ninfas del cáncer"* ("the three nymphs of cancer"), p. 509; *"las alegres fiebres"* ("the merry fevers"), p. 517; *"pequeños dolores ilesos"* ("little unhurt pains"), p. 518; *"las oscuras ninfas del cólera"* ("the dark nymphs of cholera"), p. 521; *"frescas guirnaldas de llanto"* ("fresh garlands of tears"), p. 528. There are in the New York poems at least four times as many of these examples as I have quoted. What they all have in common is the joining in one semantic unit of two or more words of antithetical value, thus creating an air of tension and ambiguity.

Of all the poetic devices used by Lorca to convey ambiguity, the most successful is probably the ambiguous symbol. That most of his symbols are ambiguous in the sense that their meanings may vary from context to context has been noted by more than one scholar.[2] What has not been noted, much less studied, is the notion that the ambiguity of his symbols is a calculated and effective way of expressing what he wanted to express. With this notion in mind, let us study the development of several of his major symbols. To gain some confidence that we have arrived at a reasonably accurate understanding of them, we will have to range through all of Lorca's poetry. All of the examples chosen for study are, however, essential to the interpretation of *Poeta en Nueva York*.

The flower called *lirio* may be a good one to start with, not because it is one

2. R. Martínez Nadal speaks of the "rich polyvalence that characterizes all the Lorcan images, metaphors and symbols." See his *El público: Amor, teatro y caballos en la obra de Federico García Lorca* (Oxford: The Dolphin Book Co., 1970), p. 208. This important study deals with several of the ambiguities discussed in this chapter. Another scholar who emphasizes the variability of Lorcan symbols is Marie Laffranque. See her *Les Idées Esthétiques . . .*, p. 222.

of the best but because it serves so well to illustrate how Lorca gradually built up the expressive potentiality of his symbols. The basic meaning of the word is "iris." In certain contexts and with certain modifiers, it may mean "lily," but in some contexts it is impossible to tell which flower is intended. One of Lorca's critics has written that in Andalusia it is associated with the color *morado*, that is, with the reddish purple of the mulberry. He has also said that it is a sign of pain and suffering.[3] One of the old maids in Lorca's play *Doña Rosita la Soltera* (1935) assigns it the value of "hope." I cite these conflicting values at this point, so that the reader may judge how misleading it could be to suppose that any one clue, even if provided by the author himself, would be sufficient to establish the meaning of a Lorcan symbol.

The first occurrence of *lirio* is found in "Balada triste" (1918); it appears in the following couplet from *Libro de poemas*:

Y vi que en vez de rosas y claveles
ella tronchaba lirios con sus manos.   (p. 191)

> And I saw that instead of roses and carnations
> she was tearing up irises with her hands.

Since this is the first appearance of the word, there are no prior contexts to help discover its meaning, which remains obscure. A few pages later it appears in a series of similes toward the end of another early poem called "El canto a la miel" (1918). Honey is described as:

Dulce como los vientres de las hembras.
Dulce como los ojos de los niños.
Dulce como las sombras de la noche.
Dulce como una voz. O como un lirio.   (p. 200)

> Sweet as the bellies of females.
> Sweet as the eyes of children.
> Sweet as the shadows of night.
> Sweet as a voice. Or an iris.

In this second example it is possible at least to be certain that *lirio* is intended to be positive. Ten pages later there occurs an example of clearly negative value:

3. See Carlos Ramos-Gil, *Claves líricas de García Lorca* (Madrid: Aguilar, 1967), pp. 143–44.

Yo *tengo sed de aromas y de risas,*
sed de cantares nuevos,
sin lunas y sin lirios,
y sin amores muertos.   (p. 211)

> I am thirsty for aromas and laughter,
> thirsty for new songs,
> without moons and without irises,
> and without dead loves.

The next three examples are also clearly negative:

¿Te [la piel de mi corazón] colgaré sobre los muros
de mi museo sentimental,
junto a los gélidos y oscuros
lirios durmientes de mi mal?   (p. 232)

> Shall I hang you [the skin of my heart] on the walls
> of my sentimental museum,
> beside the dark and frigid
> sleeping irises of my woe?

que yo sabré encenderle
sus ojos pensativos
con mis besos manchados
de lirios.   (p. 243)

> for I will know how
> to kindle her pensive eyes
> with my kisses stained
> with irises.

corazón con arroyos
y pinos,
corazón sin culebras
ni lirios.   (p. 243)

> heart with brooks
> and pines,
> heart without snakes
> or irises.

Although there remain several more examples of *lirio* in *Libro de poemas,* I cite only one more to show a shift back to the positive:

canté con los lirios canciones serenas.   (p. 281)

With irises I sang songs serene.

Perhaps all that can as yet be safely said of the examples adduced is that their meaning is variable and that those of negative import tend toward the sinister.

There are not many examples of *lirio* in the books between *Libro de poemas* and *Romancero gitano,* and it is only in this latter book that we begin to find examples of Lorca at his best in the use of this trope. One occurs in the ballad "Reyerta":

Juan Antonio el de Montilla
rueda muerto la pendiente,
su cuerpo lleno de lirios
y una granada en las sienes.
Ahora monta cruz de fuego
carretera de la muerte.   (p. 429)

> Juan Antonio from Montilla
> rolls dead down the slope,
> his body full of irises
> and a pomegranate on his temples.
> He mounts now a fiery cross
> on the highway to death.

Here the irises begin by being images: they represent the dark blood stains on a body riddled with knife wounds. But the wounds are lethal, and we realize that *lirio* has taken on associations with death. If we turn back now to the negative examples already recorded, we may fairly surmise that associations with death were already attaching themselves to some of the *lirios* in the poet's first collection of verse. This being granted, the "kisses stained with irises" express that fated union of love and death so typical of Lorca's writing. In *Llanto por Ignacio Sánchez Mejías* there is another example of *lirio* as the visual sign of a wound: in this case, the place where Ignacio was fatally gored by a bull: "*Trompa de lirio por las verdes ingles . . .*" ("Trumpet of iris along the green groins . . ."), p. 538. Here again the function of *lirio* is to represent the color of a bloody wound; *trompa* describes the shape of the wound and helps to herald its mortal effects.

Of the five instances of *lirio* in *Poeta en Nueva York*, two are of uncertain value and three are clearly negative. Here is a fragment of the context of the first negative example taken from "El niño Stanton":

Stanton, vete al bosque con tus arpas judías,
vete para aprender celestiales palabras
que duermen en los troncos, en nubes, en tortugas,

. . . .

en lirios que no duermen, en aguas que no copian,
para que aprendas, hijo, lo que tu pueblo olvida.   (p. 503)

    Stanton, go off to the forest with your jewsharps,
    go off to learn the heavenly words
    that slumber in the trunks, in clouds, in tortoises,

    . . . .

    in irises that sleep not, in waters that do not copy,
    to learn, son, what your people forget.

The "irises that sleep not" may well be the vigilant harbingers of death. The second example is from "Paisaje con dos tumbas y un perro asirio":

El aullido
es una larga lengua morada que deja
hormigas de espanto y licor de lirios.   (p. 510)

    The howl
    is a long purple tongue that leaves
    ants of fright and liquor of irises.

In the house where "the three nymphs of cancer have been dancing" the howl of the Assyrian dog leaves in its wake the agents of fright and the flavor of death. The last of the clearly negative examples is found in a verse from "Pequeño vals vienés": "*en el oscuro desván del lirio*" ("in the dark garret of irises"), p. 527; which is the repository of discarded and lifeless things.

As we shall soon see, some of Lorca's ambiguous symbols express two or more meanings that are sometimes clearly separable. The ambiguity of *lirio* is vaguer. If I have considered it less successful than some of the others, that is not because of its ambiguity. I believe that Lorca has created a deliberately ambiguous symbolic system, because what he is trying to express so often involves the disturbing emotions of conflicting intimations and premonitions. To put it another way: the psychic states he seeks to express are troubled in exactly the same double sense that turbid waters may be said to be troubled (so it is not surprising that *turbio* is a much-used item in his poetic diction). To take a pretty flower like the iris and build it into a vaguely sinister symbol is to create an expressive element appropriate to the psychic experiences that I have attempted to characterize.

Of all the ambiguous symbols in Lorca's poetry the most obsessive are the ones that bring love and death together in one way or another. In an early poem, dated August 1918, the following stanza occurs:

ver la vida y la muerte,
la síntesis del mundo,
que en espacios profundos
se miran y se abrazan.   (p. 583)

    to see life and death,
    the synthesis of the world,
    which in profound space
    gaze at each other and embrace.

And in a *gacela* of his last collection of verse, this stanza is found:

No hay noche que, al dar un beso,
no sienta las sonrisas de las gentes sin rostro,
ni hay nadie que, al tocar un recién nacido,
olvide las inmóviles calaveras del caballo.   (p. 565)

    There is no night that, on giving a kiss,
    I do not sense the smiles of the faceless people,
    nor is there anyone who, on touching a newborn child,
    forgets the motionless horse skulls.

This second example not only joins love and death but also insinuates that the fruits of love are the sustenance of death. Lorca has developed many ways of suggesting the endless intercourse of love and death. Five of the most successful symbols used to express such intercourse are: *caballo, luna, viento, manzana,* and *arena.* Although we intend to study them as effective symbols of love and death, we must note in passing that these two themes do not exhaust the possibilities of these symbols. As a matter of fact, they sometimes perform a visual rather than a symbolic function. One thinks of the high-lighted rump of the horse in the right foreground of Velázquez's "The Surrender of Breda" on reading verses like these:

mientras el cielo reluce
como la grupa de un potro.   (p. 446)

    while the sky shines
    like the croup of a colt.

Many critics have recognized the Lorcan horse as a symbol of the erotic impulses of man.[4] This value of horse is evident in so many poems (not to mention plays like *Bodas de sangre* and *La casa de Bernarda Alba*) that it scarcely requires much illustration. Let me just recall two clear examples: the neighing of the king's horses immediately before Amnon rapes his sister Thamar in the ballad bearing their name (p. 466) and the restless kicking of the white stallion before Adela gives herself to Pepe Romano in *La casa de Bernarda Alba* (pp. 1508, 1509). Once this value of *caballo* has been established, any allusion to the animal may arouse erotic meanings, and it is striking how often these meanings enter into mysterious relationships with death. A curious example is found in the poem "Crucifixión." The first verse expresses the central theme of the poem:

La luna pudo detenerse al fin por la curva blanquísima de los caballos (p. 532)

    The moon could be detained at last by the whitest curve of the horses.

Knowing that *luna* is often a symbol of death in Lorca's poetic universe, we may interpret the verse as follows: "By the grace of love was death finally detained." If this interpretation seems far-fetched, consider the following details: Before the moment represented by the words "pudo detenerse," sinister things were happening. Verses 8 and 9 run thus:

Y llegaban largos alaridos por el Sur de la noche seca.
Era que la luna quemaba con sus bujías el falo de los caballos.   (p. 532)

---

4. Probably the best study of the horse in Lorca's writings is that of Martínez Nadal in his *El público . . .*, pp. 193–233.

And long howls came on through the dry Southern night.
It was because the moon with its candles was burning the phalluses of the horses.

That is to say, death was maltreating love. Verses 30–32 signify a radical change:

Se supo el momento preciso de la salvación de nuestra vida.
Porque la luna lavó con agua
las quemaduras de los caballos.   (p. 533)

> The exact moment of the saving of our life was learned.
> Because the moon washed with water
> the horses' burns.

This reconciliation of death and love repeats the central theme of the poem and expresses the symbolic sense of the Crucifixion.

If the horse is a symbol of love and enters with that value into relationships with death, he may in his own right also symbolize death. Remember the "Caballito negro./ ¿Dónde llevas tu jinete muerto?" ("Little black horse./ Where are you taking your dead rider?"), p. 376; or the "Cien jacas caracolean./ Sus jinetes están muertos." ("A hundred ponies prance about./ Their riders are dead"), p. 315; or the black pony whose rider death awaited before reaching Cordoba, p. 380. If horse may symbolize either love or death, then its use in ambiguous contexts is an effective way to evoke both. Even when close study reveals that one of the two meanings is to be preferred in a given context, both may be stirred in the consciousness of the reader. For an example we may turn to some verses from "Romance de la pena negra":

Las piquetas de los gallos
cavan buscando la aurora,
cuando por el monte oscuro
baja Soledad Montoya.
Cobre amarillo, su carne
huele a caballo y a sombra.   (p. 436)

> The roosters' picks dig
> seeking the dawn,
> when down the dark mountain
> comes Soledad Montoya.

> Yellow copper, her flesh
> smells of horses and dusk.

Does this allusion to horses point to love or death? Perhaps the first thing it suggests is gypsy life so intimately associated with horses, but it soon becomes apparent that more is intended. When the poet asks:

Soledad, ¿por quién preguntas
sin compaña y a estas horas?   (p. 436)

> Soledad, for whom are you asking
> without company and at this hour?

She answers:

Vengo a buscar lo que busco,
mi alegría y mi persona.   (ibid.)

> I have come to seek what I seek,
> my joy and myself.

The poet's rejoinder brings us back to the value of horse:

Soledad de mis pesares,
caballo que se desboca,
al fin encuentra la mar
y se lo tragan las olas.   (ibid.)

> Soledad of my sorrows,
> the run-away horse
> finds finally the sea
> and is swallowed by the waves.

Which is to say that the run-away horse of amorous passion will be swallowed up in the sea of death. In some contexts it may not matter much which is the dominant value of horse, since both stand ready to contribute to the turbid air of sex and death that permeates verses like these from "Martirio de Santa Olalla":

Y mientras vibra confusa
pasión de crines y espadas,

el Cónsul porta en bandeja
senos ahumados de Olalla.   (p. 459)

    And while throbs a confused
    passion of horsehair and swords,
    the Consul carries on a salver
    Olalla's smoky breasts.

So far in the discussion of *caballo*, only one example from *Poeta en Nueva York* has been adduced. Despite the urban setting of a large part of this work, it contains at least twenty-three other allusions to *caballo*. Does what I have thus far said about it apply to its frequent use in *Poeta en Nueva York*? A partial answer would be that all the values so far illustrated can be found in that work also. There is at least one example that seems to be mostly visual. Smoke curling from the stacks of ocean liners seen from Battery Place may have prompted: "*Fachada de crin, de humo . . .*" ("Facade of mane, of smoke . . ."), p. 490. There are passages that typically express the poet's obsession with the inevitable commerce of love and death:

yo, poeta sin brazos, perdido
entre la multitud que vomita,
sin caballo efusivo que corte
los espesos musgos de mis sienes.   (p. 488)

    I, armless poet, lost
    among the vomiting crowd,
    without a loving horse to cut
    the thick moss from my temples.

The poet feels himself lost among the vomiting multitude without love to combat the agents of encroaching death. But there exist examples more mysterious, like the *caballo azul* (blue horse) twice mentioned in *Poeta en Nueva York*. To these we will have to return at the proper time. Meanwhile, it is probably true to say that whatever the dominant value of *caballo* may be in a given context, its power to recall the themes of love and death will always hover in the background ready to contribute to the expressive ambiguity sought by the poet.

    Turning now to the symbol *luna*, I have already quoted two passages in which the moon carried the suggestion of death. The lines containing the first negative example of *lirio* also contained the negative moon: "*sin lunas y sin lirios,/ y sin amores muertos*" ("without moons and without irises,/ and without dead loves"), p. 211. And in the poem "Crucifixión" we saw the moon of death in conflict with the horse of love. The poet once wrote that death disguises itself as love (p. 670). When it does, the moon may reflect or assume the form of a seductive female. In the ballad "Thamar y Amnón," for example:

Amnón estaba mirando
la luna redonda y baja,
y vio en la luna los pechos
durísimos de su hermana.   (p. 465)

    Amnon was watching
    the moon round and low,
    and saw in the moon
    the hard breasts of his sister.

In the "Romance de la luna, luna" the moon appears thus:

En el aire conmovido
mueve la luna sus brazos
y enseña, lúbrica y pura,
sus senos de duro estaño.   (p. 425)

    In the commotion of the wind
    the moon waves her arms
    and shows, lubric and pure,
    her breasts of hard tin.

Although the moon is usually hostile to love, on rare occasions it may humble itself before love, as in this verse from *Poeta en Nueva York*: "*por los palomares donde la luna se pone plana bajo el gallo*" ("around the dovecotes where the moon lies flat beneath the cock"), p. 474. Its frequent ambiguity is well illustrated in this stanza from one of the final poems of *Poeta en Nueva York*:

Te quiero, te quiero, te quiero,
con la butaca y el libro muerto,
por el melancólico pasillo,
en el oscuro desván del lirio,
en nuestra cama de la luna
y en la danza que sueña la tortuga.   (p. 527)

I love you, I love you, I love you,
with the armchair and the dead book,
along the melancholy corridor,
in the dark garret of the iris,
in our bed of the moon
and in the dance the tortoise dreams.

Who can tell whether *"cama de la luna"* is bridal bed or death bed? It is a
good guess that the poet wanted that question unanswered.

Although the negative moon plays a prominent role in most of Lorca's
works, it probably appears more frequently in *Poeta en Nueva York* than in
any similar number of pages in any other work. If it appears there at least
three dozen times, it is surely because death is so dominant a theme in that
book. We shall see further examples of it at work as we proceed with the
study of other symbols.

Among the natural elements that acquire symbolic value in Lorca's poetry,
one of the more frequent ones is the wind in its various manifestations: *aire*
(wind), *brisa* (breeze), *huracán* (hurricane), *vendaval* (gale), *viento* (wind).
The first poem in Lorca's first collection of poems begins with these verses:

Viento del Sur,
moreno, ardiente,
llegas sobre mi carne,
trayéndome semilla
de brillantes
miradas, empapado
de azahares.   (p. 173)

Wind of the South,
dark, ardent,
you come upon my flesh,
bringing me seed
of brilliant glances,
laden with orange blossoms.

Generally faithful to this beginning, the winds that blow in the poet's works
are charged with sensuality, most often of the erotic kind. In one of his well-
known lectures, he spoke of the strange materialization of the wind in the
poetry of "deep song," of how it appears there in the guise of a personage. The
same thing happens in his own poetry. For example:

La niña de bello rostro
está cogiendo aceituna.
El viento, galán de torres,
la prende por la cintura.   (p. 381)

> The girl with the beautiful face
> is gathering olives.
> The wind, wooer of towers,
> catches her by the waist.

The most explicit case of the wind as an erotic character is found in the ballad called "Preciosa y el aire." Preciosa is coming along a path playing her tambourine when the wind accosts her with lewd words. Four verses are enough to describe the ensuing situation:

Preciosa tira el pandero
y corre sin detenerse.
El viento-hombrón la persigue
con una espada caliente.   (p. 427)

> Preciosa throws her tambourine aside
> and runs without stopping.
> The big man-wind pursues her
> with a burning sword.

The wind may be the bearer of mortal omens:

El grito deja en el viento
una sombra de ciprés.   (p. 303)

> The cry leaves in the wind
> a shadow of cypress.

More commonly it alludes to love somehow bound to death. Provisionally, death may give way to love, as in the poem titled "Huerto de marzo":

Mi manzano
tiene ya sombra y pájaros.
¡Qué brinco de mi sueño
de la luna al viento!   (p. 417)

My apple tree
has shade now and birds.
How my dream leaps
from the moon to the wind!

The advent of spring prompts the poet's dream to skip from death to love. But love generally follows the opposite course:

Mañana los amores serán rocas y el Tiempo
una brisa que viene dormida por las ramas. (p. 525)

> Tomorrow the love affairs will be rocks and time
> a breeze that comes through the branches asleep.

The ultimate destiny of the amorous breeze is a rendezvous with the worm of death; so it is proclaimed in the *Oda al Santísimo Sacramento del Altar*:

Porque tu signo expresa la brisa y el gusano.
Punto de unión y cita del siglo y el minuto. (p. 632)

> Because your sign expresses the breeze and the worm.
> Place of union and rendezvous of the century and the minute.

In one form or another, the wind appears in *Poeta en Nueva York* more than three dozen times. Among these instances, there are illustrations of all the meanings shown above and more besides. Occasionally, it is strongly visual, as in *"un huracán de negras palomas"* ("a hurricane of black pigeons"), p. 497. It is slyly ambiguous in verses like *"y el viento acecha troncos descuidados"* ("and the wind stalks careless trunks"), p. 499. When accompanied by the word *oscuro* (dark), it may point to inverted love: *"y el aire era una manzana oscura"* ("and the wind was a dark apple"), p. 511. Later it will be necessary to look at some of these examples in larger contexts.

Among the fruits converted into symbols, one of the clearest and most constant is the apple. In 1920 Lorca used this symbol in at least two poems. Both are found in *Libro de poemas*. The first begins like this:

Junta tu boca con la mía,
¡oh Estrella la gitana!
bajo el oro solar del mediodía
morderé la manzana. (p. 209)

Join your red mouth to mine,
Oh Estrella the Gypsy!
Under the solar gold of noon
I will bite the apple.

If this is quite clear, the second example is even more so:

La manzana es lo carnal,
fruta esfinge del pecado.   (p. 258)

The apple is what's carnal,
the sphinx-like fruit of sin.

Perhaps it should be noted that whereas the symbol is explicitly defined, what the symbol ultimately stands for is given the inscrutable character of a sphinx. Since the apple often represents carnal love, it will not surprise us to see it in the company of the other symbols already reviewed:

Pronto se vio que la luna
era una calavera de caballo
y el aire una manzana oscura.   (p. 511)

Soon it was seen that the moon
was the skull of a horse
and the wind a dark apple.

This dark apple, twice quoted already, may also appear as a green apple. In the brief poem called "Susto en el comedor" the poetic voice says to a girl (represented by the color rose):

Quise las manzanas verdes.
No las manzanas rosadas . . .   (p. 398)

I wanted the green apples.
Not the rosy apples . . .

In Christian art an apple in the hands of Christ often symbolizes salvation. Whether or not there are echoes of this meaning in Lorca is not certain. The following example may echo this meaning; at any rate, it makes of symbolic apples a refuge from death:

Quiero dormir el sueño de las manzanas,
alejarme del tumulto de los cementerios.   (p. 563)

I wish to sleep the sleep of apples,
to withdraw from the tumult of the cemeteries.

In *Poeta en Nueva York* the apple symbol is used only eleven times, but that is enough to render useful some preliminary acquaintance with its meaning.

Once the reader has been fully persuaded that Lorca uses ambiguous symbols deliberately to express the ambiguities of psychic experience, the reader ceases to be troubled by his inability to fix one or two stable meanings for each of the symbols he encounters. The ambiguities of the poet's rhetoric begin to seem both natural and effective. For a final example of such symbols, we may turn our attention to *arena* (sand).[5] The first time it appears in his poetry is in "La guitarra" from *Poema del cante jondo*. The example occurs right after the guitar is said to weep for distant things:

Arena del Sur caliente
que pide camelias blancas.   (p. 297)

> Sand of the burning South
> that asks for white camellias.

In its first use, then, sand is associated with some as yet unidentified southern land, a land of heat and probably passion, a suitable setting for romantic, perhaps impossible, love. In his "Oda a Walt Whitman" the poet sets "north" and "sand" in contrast: *"rubios del norte, negros de la arena"* (blonds of the North, blacks of the sand"), p. 524; so that once more *arena* suggests the South, which from the perspective of Spain and by virtue of the mention of Negroes evokes Africa. In verses designed to recall the sensual nature of blacks, we find another example of *arena*: *"y patinan lúbricos por agua y arenas"* (and they slip lubricous over water and sands"), p. 477. In the "Danza de la Muerte" of *Poeta en Nueva York* the African mask that advances on New York is accompanied by varied portents of retribution. Here is one example:

El mascarón. ¡Mirad el mascarón!
¡Arena, caimán y miedo sobre Nueva York!   (p. 485)

> The mask. Look at the mask!
> Sand, alligator and fear over New York!

5. It is surprising how unequivocally certain critics state without adducing any evidence the symbolic meaning of certain words used by Lorca. A recent example is Betty Jean Craige, who affirms that Lorca uses "sand" to represent consciousness. See her *Lorca's Poet in New York* (Lexington: The University of Kentucky Press, 1977), p. 56.

Once more sand is associated with Africa, although in this instance its sign is patently negative.

One learns to expect that the symbolic value of sand will fluctuate between positive and negative poles. A little poem titled "Memento [Mori]" from *Poema del cante jondo* begins with these verses:

Cuando yo me muera
enterradme con mi guitarra
bajo la arena.   (p. 323)

> When I die
> bury me with my guitar
> under the sand.

Since these words express the poet's wish for himself, we must assume that *arena* is here used positively. The guitar stands for his devotion to music, the sand carries the expressive potentialities of a passionate Southland. Still, even in this early poem, sand has entered the sphere of death, as it is so many times destined to do. Sometimes clearly, as in these verses from *Llanto por Ignacio Sánchez Mejías*:

Dile a la luna que venga,
que no quiero ver la sangre
de Ignacio sobre la arena.   (p. 539)

> Tell the moon to come,
> for I do not wish to see the blood
> of Ignacio on the sand.

Or as it appears repeatedly in a later poem titled "Canción de la muerte pequeña." Two brief stanzas will suffice as examples:

Me encontré con la muerte.
Prado mortal de tierra.
Una muerte pequeña.

. . . .

Catedral de ceniza.
Luz y noche de arena.
Una muerte pequeña.   (p. 640)

    I happened upon death.
    Mortal meadow of earth.
    A little death.

    .   .   .   .   .   .

    Cathedral of ashes.
    Light and night of sand.
    A little death.

Sometimes the value of sand is less clear, as in these verses from "Romance de la Guardia Civil Española":

Jorobados y nocturnos,
por donde animan ordenan
silencios de goma oscura
y miedos de fina arena.   (p. 453)

    Hunchbacked and nocturnal,
    wherever they stir things up
    they order silences of dark rubber
    and fears of fine sand.

Is this the sand of their regular beach patrols or the fine sand of an hourglass about to run out?

The mortal blood of Sánchez Mejías on the sand tends to make it (the sand) an accomplice of death, but this kind of association is not the only path that leads to the sand of death. The sterile nature of sand belongs to the world of common knowledge. Hence it is easy to understand why sand is present in the song that one of the washwomen in *Yerma* sings of a barren woman:

Pero ¡ay de la casada seca!
¡Ay de la que tiene los pechos de arena!   (p. 1310)

    But woe betide the withered wife!
    Woe to her whose breasts are sand!

If the aura of death often hovers over sand, it is both because of its nature and because the poet has chosen to endow it with mortal associations. This is the double approach to symbol building of Lorca at his best. Ordinarily starting with a concrete reality, preferably visual, he gradually builds its complex symbolic possibilities.

Let us look now at some examples of *arena* in erotic contexts. An example, which illustrates superbly the technique just described, may be found in the ballad of "La casada infiel." Consider the following verses:

Sucia de besos y arena,
yo me la llevé del río.
Con el aire se batían
las espadas de los lirios.   (p. 435)

> Dirty with kisses and sand,
> I brought her from the river.
> The swords of the irises
> were fighting with the wind.

Since the river bank was the couch of love, how simple and direct it is to characterize the unfaithful wife as "dirty with kisses and sand." But is this all the poet meant to express or did he wish to suggest that love and death had grappled once more? Verses 3 and 4 may provide an answer. At first glance, they seem to describe only a visual experience: the sword-shaped leaves of the irises are contending with the wind. But when we remember that in Lorca's poetry the wind may be erotic and irises may augur death, one sees that verses 3 and 4 neatly confirm the proposed interpretation of verse 1. The love of the unfaithful married woman is not only literally contaminated with sand but also with faithlessness and death.

Arena is used some twelve times in *Poeta en Nueva York.* Among the examples of *arena* so far displayed, two were taken from that book. Let us look at two more. In the love poem called "Tu infancia en Menton" the poet describes the (probably male) beloved in these verses:

Tu cintura de arena sin sosiego
atiende solo rastros que no escalan.   (p. 476)

> Your waist of restless sand
> heeds only trails that do not climb.

What does a waist of restless sand suggest: passion, dalliance, sterility? Perhaps all three, but let us consider the third possibility. It fits in with a notion more than once expressed by the poet: the fruits of heterosexual love are fated to become the fodder of death. Inverted love is barren. It may be looked upon, then, as having the virtue of cheating death out of its usual fare. Another example in which to consider this possibility is given in the poem "Cielo vivo." Some verses that express how the poet would satisfy his quest for amorous joy are these:

pero me iré al primer paisaje de humedades y latidos
para entender que lo que busco tendrá su blanco de alegría
cuando yo vuele mezclado con el amor y las arenas.   (p. 500)

> but I will away to the first landscape of heartbeats and damp places
> to understand that what I seek will have its target of joy
> when I can fly mingled with love and sands.

This return to some primal landscape may be a return to a time of beginnings before certain social taboos had emerged. If in this context "flying" stands for freedom, it is freedom to love according to his nature. The sands are meant to suggest sterile love, which is to say, love between men. There are many signs that the poet was moving toward ever greater frankness of expression on this subject. An example that "Cielo vivo" calls to mind is these verses from the "Oda a Walt Whitman":

El cielo tiene playas donde evitar la vida
y hay cuerpos que no deben repetirse en la aurora.   (p. 525)

> Heaven has shores where life may be avoided
> and there are bodies which should not be repeated in the dawn.

To sum up, we may say that Lorca gradually endows *arena* with at least the following meanings: South, Africa, heat, passion, sensuality, sterility, death, and homosexual love. By the time he had written the poems collected in *Poeta en Nueva York*, all of these expressive possibilities were available. But merely to say this does not adequately account for this aspect of Lorca's art. The clusters of meanings that attach to his most successful symbols are deliberately ambiguous, because only so could he hope to express the tensions and contradictions of his psychic experience. In this regard it may be relevant to remember some of the notions recorded in chapter 1. There we saw that Lorca had written that he was seeking the truth of mistaken things, a poetry that would combine beauty and horror, that would express pure emotion, that would be freed from reality and logical control but would obey a tremendous poetic logic of its own. One may think of the artistic creation that sprang from these principles as a verbal structure where words interact with their linguistic environment (context) more than with the world of real things, or, as some critics might put it, where the signifiers count for more than the signified. In such a virtual world, expressed in the rhetoric we have examined, it is possible to achieve powerful emotional effects without much explicit meaning. Perhaps a good illustration of such effects is found in the last two lines of the last stanza of the "Romance de la Guardia Civil Española":

¡Oh ciudad de los gitanos!
¿Quién te vio y no te recuerda?
Que te busquen en mi frente.
Juego de luna y arena.   (p. 457)

    Oh city of the Gypsies!
    Who has seen you and remembers you not?
    Let them seek you on my forehead.
    Play of moon and sand.

To the experienced reader of Lorca, how expressive is that "play of moon and sand."

3

First look at *Poeta en Nueva York*

In an autobiographical note written shortly after the New York trip Lorca declared: "It can be said that the trip to New York enriched and changed the work of the poet, since it was the first time he confronted a new world" (p. 1698). Although these words carry much truth, it is also true that in both poetic style and content *Poeta en Nueva York* contains much that is present in his earlier works. Abundant evidence of this fact will be offered in the course of this study.

In a 1931 interview about his New York experience Lorca observed in the telegraphic style that sometimes comes out of interviews: "I have prepared four books. Of theater. Of poetry. And of New York impressions, which might be called The City, personal interpretation, impersonal abstraction, without time or place in that city-world. . . . It puts my poetic world in contact with the poetic world of New York" (p. 1699). One of the tasks before us is to try to define the relation between those two worlds. In the meantime let us note that the poet is conscious of two worlds: his own and that of New York.

The second made him think of calling his new work *The City*,[1] a title that would invite the reader to see New York as the prototype of the monstrous dehumanized city of the contemporary world, and, as a matter of fact, one senses that the poet did intend to generalize his apocalyptic vision of New York to the Western world.[2] Nevertheless, he finally decided not to bestow that title on his new book, and it was a good decision. If we assume that the two worlds can for convenience be used as labels to classify two kinds of poems, those dealing largely with New York and those dealing mainly with the poet's private concerns, it becomes clear that the second category is by far the more abundant. But this classification is crude. The new book is truly about the poet *in* New York (and a few other places in America).

It may be helpful to undertake our first look at *Poeta en Nueva York* with a kind of rough inventory. The poet divided his work into ten major sections of uneven length. The first section, called "Poemas de la soledad en Columbia University," consists of four poems: "Vuelta de paseo," "1910 (Intermedio)," "Fábula y rueda de los tres amigos," and "Tu infancia en Menton." They amount to 148 verses of unequal length.

The first thing that strikes the reader about this opening section is that it has so little to do specifically with New York. It is true that in the first poem the poet uses some impressions gathered on a walk in New York. What matters is not the walk but what the poet creates in solitude with the impressions of the walk after it is over. Although this is not the place to offer detailed interpretations of individual poems, I must offer an interpretation of this one to guide us in our preliminary exploration of the book. Since the poem is short, I will reproduce it whole:

1   *Asesinado por el cielo,*
     entre las formas que van hacia la sierpe
3   *y las formas que buscan el cristal,*
     dejaré crecer mis cabellos.

5   *Con el árbol de muñones que no canta*
     y el niño con el blanco rostro de huevo.

---

1. Marie Laffranque seems to believe that *La ciudad* was not intended to be the title of the collection of New York poems. See her *Les Idées Esthétiques*, p. 270. However, the poet's brother, Francisco, confirmed to me, *viva voce*, that he thought it was. Another title that Lorca appears to have considered is *Introdución a la muerte*. See R. Martínez Nadal, *Federico García Lorca: Autógrafos I* (Oxford: The Dolphin Book Co., 1975), p. xxxiv.
   2. See Fusero, p. 294.

7 Con los animalitos de cabeza rota
  y el agua harapienta de los pies secos.
9 Con todo lo que tiene cansancio sordomudo
  y mariposa ahogada en el tintero.

11 Tropezando con mi rostro distinto de cada día.
  ¡Asesinado por el cielo!   (p. 471)

1 Having been assassinated by heaven,
  between the forms that go toward the serpent
3 and the forms that seek the crystal,
  I'll let my hair grow.

5 With the tree whose stumps sing not
  and the child with the egg's white face.

7 With the little broken-headed animals
  and the tattered water of dry feet.

9 With all that holds deaf and dumb fatigue
  and butterfly drowned in the inkwell.

11 Stumbling upon my different face each day.
  Having been assassinated by heaven!

Much of what becomes symbolic in Lorca's poetry begins as visual impression. What could be the visual origins of verses 2 and 3? One of the most insistent visual impressions experienced by Lorca in New York was that of the endless batteries of windows. From the street level one's eyes may be drawn upward by row upon row of luminous glass (*el cristal*). Seen in horizontal perspective, the streets may appear long and narrow like serpents. The visual origin of verse 5 is a heavily pruned tree whose truncated branches resemble amputated limbs; they are songless because of the absence of birds. As images picked up in the street, neither the white egg-faced child nor the little animals with broken heads need explanation. Verse 8 is less obvious. A plausible interpretation is that the "tattered water of dry feet" represents the way the poet saw at foot level the flowing movement of anonymous crowds.[3] It does not matter too much if some of the suggestions just recorded are not

3. C. Marcilly presents an interpretation much like this. See his *Ronde et Fable de la Solitude à New York* (Paris: Ediciones Hispano-Americanas, 1962), p. 10.

entirely accurate. The point to be established is the concrete visual beginnings of so much of Lorca's poetry.

There is no hint of anecdote in the poem except whatever slight anecdote may be implied by the walk now over. The discursive structure of the verses is minimal. The only complete sentence in the entire poem is distributed between verses 1 and 4: "Having been assassinated by heaven,/ I'll let my hair grow." This is the central theme of the poem, and these verses are not the only ones in which the poet speaks of his own murder as of a past event. For example, in the third poem of the section we are now examining, he writes:

Cuando se hundieron las formas puras
bajo el cri cri de las margaritas,
comprendí que me habían asesinado.   (p. 475)

> When the pure forms collapsed
> under the cri cri of the daisies,
> I understood that they had murdered me.

In the light of the actual murder of Lorca in 1936, these and other similar statements may seem eerie. Still, most readers are probably unwilling to assume that in 1929 Lorca was consciously foretelling the manner of his own death. What, then, was he trying to express? To find an answer, we must first consider the verb *asesinar*. In addition to its common first sense, it has two figurative meanings, which originate as hyperbolic expressions of afflictions of lesser magnitude than murder. The two figurative meanings may be summed up in the phrases "to betray" and "to plague sorely." Whether in the poem *asesinar* conveys its literal meaning "to murder" or one of its figurative meanings, it is important to remember that the verb refers to a deliberate action. One may be killed accidentally; assassination is always intentional. Furthermore, assassination usually implies treachery, something not commonly considered compatible with heaven's decrees. The poet is talking, then, about his fate: he has been condemned (and betrayed) by heaven's will, from which there is no escape. This being accepted, he will let his hair grow, as all men must do when they die.[4]

By turning our attention back to verses 2 and 3, we may now gain a clearer view of the poet's doom. Whatever the exact value of *asesinar* may be, the poet is doomed to suffer it between the forms that go toward the serpent and the forms that seek the crystal. In other words, he feels himself

4. In Christian symbolism to let one's hair grow long was to do penance. See George Ferguson, *Signs and Symbols in Christian Art* (New York: Oxford University Press, 1966), p. 47.

condemned to suffer his fate caught in the tensions of such opposing forces as may be implied by serpent and crystal. Although Lorca does not encourage us to find precise solutions to the "riddle of the image," we may assume that serpent and crystal stand for something like man's lower impulses and his higher aspirations.[5] If so, the verbs used with serpent and crystal are expressive: the forms "go" toward the lower and "seek" the higher.

After the stanza we have been examining come three distichs, each introduced by the preposition "with." They contain the images that are with the poet as he struggles to express the fateful intimation just described. They are the images of the mutilated tree, the absent birds, the anemic child, the dead animals, the anonymous crowd, and the butterfly drowned in an inkwell. The poet is accompanied, then, by organisms that are dead or mutilated or that somehow are prevented from fulfilling themselves. Perhaps the dominant note, summed up in the third distich, is the failure of expression. The verses recall the weariness of neither hearing nor speaking and the butterfly drowned in the inkwell. The butterfly of the human spirit (psyche) is stifled by the medium (ink) through which it strives to express itself.[6] In the final distich the poet records the finding of his own different face each day. The verb used (*tropezar*) gives us to understand that what he finds is found merely by chance. Unsure of his own true identity and beset by the disturbing images we have enumerated, he confirms with exclamation marks his heaven-willed doom.

"Back from a walk" is not dated. It is probably one of the early poems written

5. Juan Larrea assigns transcendental values to these symbols: "Assassinated, in effect, by celestial design, as we are seeing, and executed by the always barbarous executioners of sentences; torn between the two halves of Spain, that diabolical half that inclines toward the earth-bound serpent, and that other popular, divine, new-world-like half that seeks the crystal, the transparence of the light, appropriate to the sky (heaven), peculiar to conscious life" (*España Peregrina* [1940], 1:255).

6. On more than one occasion, Lorca expressed the deadly effect of printer's ink. Consider this stanza from a poem called "Encrucijada" (1920):

¡Oh, qué dolor el tener
versos en la lejanía
de la pasión, y el cerebro
todo manchado de tinta!   (p. 252)

    Oh, what sorrow to have
    verses so removed
    from passion, and one's brain
    all stained with ink.

Or this sentence from a 1927 letter to Jorge Guillén: "I am not interested in seeing my poems definitively dead . . . I mean published" (p. 1615).

in New York,[7] but, whether it is or not, we must assume that Lorca chose it to stand first in his new book. If we cannot know the reasons that prompted him to do so, we can advance some reasons for considering the choice a good one. With its spare, disjointed style devoid of sensual appeal, it sets the tone for a work intended to mark a radical change from the kind of poetry that had made Lorca famous; it introduces at once the perennial theme of death but this time in the context of the unresolved tensions that were tormenting him when he made his New York journey; above all, it exhibits the dominant modes by which the poet placed, to use his own words, his poetic world in contact with the poetic world of New York.

Having examined in some detail the poem Lorca selected to open his new book, I will resume my rough inventory. The three poems that constitute the rest of section 1 have nothing to do with New York. In them the poet returns in memory to earlier times. The poem titled "1910 (Interlude)" records some of the images caught by the eyes of a child. They are the then-not-understood signs of what for the man would become symbols of evil and death and love and useless, discarded things. The backward glance yields no consolation, only lost innocence, emptiness, and the sorrow of now unpeopled places. The next poem, "Fable and Round of the Three Friends," is one of the most complicated and obscure of the whole collection.[8] Still, it is safe to say that it evokes youthful friendships that were ultimately disappointing, perhaps in part because the friends did not understand the poet's art. Like some of Lorca's other poems, this one too is haunted by the poet's own death. The final poem of the section, "Your Childhood in Menton," is a love poem addressed by the poet to an unidentified *tu* (thou) whose gender is never unequivocally revealed but who seems to be male. It expresses the double anguish of a love that was both individually rejected and socially taboo. In sum, it seems fair to affirm that section 1 gives poetic expression to the principal elements of the emotional crisis that motivated the escape from Spain to the New World.

Section 2, called "Los negros," consists of three long poems totaling 185 verses. "Norma y paraíso de los negros" is the first one. It characterizes the blacks as hating the abstract, the formal, the regulated; and as loving the natural, the spontaneous, the sensual. The next poem is "Oda al rey de Harlem." It is the longest poem of the three and the one that best expresses

7. Daniel Eisenberg writes of a draft dated 6 Sept. 1929. See his *Poeta en Nueva York: Historia* . . ., p. 211.

8. The fullest attempt to explicate this poem is probably that of Marcilly, *Ronde et Fable* . . ., pp. 21–37.

the suffering of the blacks trapped in an alien culture. It launches what will become, as the book progresses, a powerful indictment of New York, and it contains the first hints of impending retribution. The final poem, "Iglesia abandonada," bears the subtitle "Balada de la Gran Guerra." Actually it has very little to do with war and nothing at all with the blacks. It laments the loss of a son, who turns out to be the boy the poet was at the time of World War I. The son appears under many guises representing his inconstant and troubled heart, whose most important loss is implied in the title: abandoned church.[9]

Section 3, "Calles y sueños," is by far the longest of the ten sections (362 verses). It consists of the following nine poems: "Danza de la muerte," "Paisaje de la multitud que vomita," "Paisaje de la multitud que orina," "Asesinato," "Navidad en el Hudson," "Ciudad sin sueño," "Panorama ciego de Nueva York," "Nacimiento de Cristo," and "La Aurora." On the surface all nine of these poems appear to be mainly about New York. They combine clearly recognizable visual impressions of New York with phantasmagorical images calculated to express the poet's reaction to the suffering and evil of the chaotic city. But beneath the surface of some of them, one senses the poet's personal preoccupations, and in at least three of them he is present in his own first person.

The hints of retribution registered in the "Ode to the King of Harlem" are advanced more forcefully and less obscurely in the "Dance of Death" led by an African mask to a Wall Street soon to be destroyed both by men (rifles) and Nature (jungle vines). The poet pictures himself on a terrace struggling with the moon (death) and aware of breezes with long wings knocking on the ashy windows of Broadway, which is to say, aware of intrusions upon his New York experience by passions born in Spain. The next two titles, "Landscape of the Vomiting Multitude" and "Landscape of the Urinating Multitude," provide an adequate notion of the poet's reaction to the motley crowds of Coney Island at dusk and Battery Place at night. At first glance they appear to be only nightmarish visions, landscapes of nausea; a closer reading reveals one of the poet's most intimate preoccupations. The first poem is dominated by a vast and active female presence, which is obviously disturbing to the poet and against which he defends himself with a look emanating from the dark waves (of forbidden love). The wave symbol appears again in the last line of

9. In a letter written to his friend Jorge Zalamea the year before he went to New York, the poet had already used the phrase: "my poor little heart (this wretched son of mine)," p. 1666.

the second poem, this time characterized as never-repeated waves, which is to say, love that is not reproductive.

The fourth poem, called "Murder," records a fragment of conversation overheard at dawn on Riverside Drive. The conversation bears witness to yet another "violent attack of the moon." The fifth poem appears to be an evocation of the grey desolation of Christmas on the Hudson, but in the end the grey emptiness of New York with its great river and the sharp angles (*aristas*) of its geometric architecture are made to express the bitter loneliness and despair of the poet. The second verse mentions a beheaded sailor who in the fourth-from-the-last verse becomes the poet himself beheaded by the cutting edge of a forbidden love. This is the third time the poet has pictured himself as in some way killed. The promise of Nativity is reversed.

The nightmare visions of New York imbued with the poet's own bitter thoughts and emotions become more and more chaotic in the second half of "Streets and Dreams." "Sleepless City" begins with a verse that runs: "*No duerme nadie por el cielo. Nadie, nadie.*" ("Nobody sleeps in the sky. Nobody. Nobody."), p. 492. Perhaps the visual beginnings of this poem are those skyscraper windows whose lights burn all night in the sky. In any case, the poet evokes a sleepless city whose vigilance is attuned to death and suffering. Despite death itself, there is neither dream nor forgetfulness, only living flesh driven to self-reproduction. Briefly the poet glimpses more attractive prospects only to end his poem with "*las copas falsas, el veneno y la calavera de los teatros*" ("the false goblets, the poison and the theaters' skull"), p. 494, which seems to refer to false friends and the disappointment and vanity of the theaters.

The seventh poem is "Blind Panorama of New York." If the visual promise of the word "panorama" is cancelled by its modifier "blind," one must suppose that the panorama presented by the poem is an inner one concerned with psychic rather than visual prospects. Such is the case: the poem expresses preoccupations with the blind forces of love and death in the context of (traditional) social conventions. The last two and a half verses affirm again the primacy of procreation:

> *Aquí solo existe la Tierra.*
> *La tierra con sus puertas de siempre*
> *que llevan al rubor de los frutos.*   (p. 496)

> Here only the Earth exists.
> The earth with its doors of forever
> which lead to the blush of the fruits.

If this vision of human life was caught in New York, its applicability is not peculiar to that city.

It is difficult to imagine what real images of a snow-covered Manhattan at the first approach of dawn inspired the oneiric vision projected by the eighth poem, "Birth of Christ," with its assembly of unlikely animals: white dogs stretched out in the snow, ants, wolves, and toads in green bonfires, and a bull dreaming (of its own statue?). The next to the last stanza presents the weeping Christ-child with a three on his forehead lying on the hay where St. Joseph sees three bronze thorns (the three nails of the Crucifixion). We may assume that the two threes recall the passion and death of Christ, which ended when he rose on the third day. Characteristically, birth is already marked for death.[10] Only the last stanza ties the poem directly to Manhattan:

La nieve de Manhattan empuja los anuncios
y lleva gracia pura por las falsas ojivas.
Sacerdotes idiotas y querubes de pluma
van detrás de Lutero por las altas esquinas.   (p. 496)

> Manhattan's snow rests heavy on the advertisements
> and carries pure grace through the false Gothic arches.
> Idiot priests and feathered cherubs
> follow Luther around the high corners.

It looks as though the birth of Christ, seen from Manhattan, offers little cause for rejoicing.

With "Dawn," the ninth and final poem of this section, we emerge from the obscure imagery of dreams into a clearer, if no less forlorn, vision of the great city with its dirt, materialism, injustice, rootless knowledge, and hopeless suffering. From "Dance of Death" to "Dawn" there is a certain temporal progression. At least part of "Dance of Death" occurs at night. The next five poems are either fully nocturnal or they represent dusk (*anochecer*) or predawn (*madrugada*). No particular time is specified in "Blind Panorama of New York" and "Birth of Christ." "Dawn" concludes the section on a note of despair doubly poignant, because even dawn conveys no promise of a better day.

Section 4, called "Poemas del lago Edem Mills," consists of only two poems

10. Lorca had already entertained this vision of the child Jesus before he left Spain for New York. At the end of a letter to his friend, Sebastian Gasch, he wrote of the emotion aroused in him by "the child Jesus abandoned at the entrance of Bethlehem, with the whole germ of the crucifixion already latent under the straw of his cradle" (p. 1657).

totaling eighty verses. The second one is dated 24 August 1929, at Eden Mills, Vermont, and it is likely that both poems were written at about that time. In the pastoral landscape of northern Vermont, the poet forgets for a while the frenzy of New York but not to achieve the peace often associated with pastoral scenes. In the first of the two poems, "Poema doble del lago Edem," he addresses his earlier voice, a voice that once flowed with roses and was ignorant of the bitter juices. But what torments the poet is not so much the contrast of the double temporal perspective as the inner conflict between love of woman and love of man. He cries out for freedom to love in his own human way, but he senses that death will seek him out where his body floats between balanced opposites, which reminds the attentive reader of the first poem of the collection with its bald statement that the poet was murdered between the forms that go toward the serpent and those that seek the crystal. The second poem is "Cielo vivo." Despite the obscurity of some of the verses, it is reasonably clear that it too is about the kind of love that would satisfy the poet's quest for amorous joy. He describes it as flying mingled with love and sand, that is, compounded of love and sterility, which states again the theme of love without issue.

Section 5, "En la cabaña del Farmer," contains three poems totaling 112 verses. The first poem, "El niño Stanton," and the third, "Niña ahogada en el pozo," are, as Professor del Río found occasion to point out, based on the poet's impressions and experiences in rural New York State, but the anecdotes they appear to incorporate are imagined. In the first one the poet personifies cancer prowling menacingly about the cabin where Stanton lived. In the third the poet imagines a little girl drowned in the forever still waters of a well.[11] The second poem, titled simply "Vaca," is the fantastic account of the death of a cow. In Lorca's poetry the cow frequently stands for the female element in nature and is usually presented as a suffering victim. All three poems express the poet's reactions to the unrelenting and unmotivated presence of death among innocent victims.

Section 6 is called "Introducción a la muerte: Poemas de la soledad en Vermont," and is composed of five poems totaling 226 verses. The first poem is "Muerte." In it the poet turns his attention from death as an unexplained occurrence to the nature of death. The poem describes the struggle of things animate and inanimate to be what they are not; only passage through the arch of death is effortless. The poet represents himself as seeking and being

11. See del Río's Introduction to Belitt's translation of *Poet in New York*, pp. xxxvi–xxxvii.

a fallen angel (seraph of flames) along the eaves, that is, along the fringes of human society. What the poem seems to suggest is that a personally chosen fulfillment requires great effort, while death comes without effort.

The second poem, "Nocturno del hueco," consists of two parts. In the first part the poet addresses a lost love—a love whose sex remains ambiguous—to lament that all things have passed away, leaving behind only the empty places (*huecos*) they once occupied. The poet himself seems to speak from the shores of death, since he refers to his own void in the air.[12] If there is a glimmer of hope in this lover's lament for things now gone forever, it may be contained in the ambiguous final stanza of part 2. Twice in part 2 he represents his absent self (*mi hueco*) accompanied by the whitest void of a horse. In the final stanza line 2 seems to deny hope while line 3 may allow it:

Yo.
No hay siglo nuevo ni luz reciente.
Solo un caballo azul y una madrugada. (p. 509)

    I.
There is no new century nor recent light.
Only a blue horse and an early dawn.

Nothing certain is known about the blue horse in Lorca's poetry, and we have already seen that early morning hours do not necessarily augur a promising day. What hope there may be, then, is highly problematical.

According to Angel del Río, the next poem, "Paisaje con dos tumbas y un perro asirio," was inspired by the landscape of Shandaken in the Catskills.[13] On the farm where Lorca stayed there was an enormous, half-blind dog and a farmer with a cancerous sore. The poem expresses the irrational terror produced by these circumstances in a nightmare vision combining the familiar elements of love and death.

The fourth poem, "Ruina," portrays love and death as urgent forces in conflict. The poet and his love must quickly seek their dreamless profile (realize themselves), because death will not wait and there is no future. The fifth and final poem is called "Luna y panorama de los insectos: Poema de amor." Although what matters in life is love, in the end only the moon (death) and the insects remain. Four of the five poems comprising "Introduction to Death" are in some sense love poems. One of the bitter ways death manifests

12. Martínez Nadal makes this point in his *El público*, p. 114.
13. See his already cited Introduction, p. xxxvii.

itself is in the destruction of love, but this can be said another way: it is death that lends urgency and value to love.

In early editions of *Poeta en Nueva York* section 7, called "Vuelta a la ciudad," consisted of only two poems: "New York: Oficina y denuncia" and "Cemeterio judío"; but in Ben Belitt's translation of the book the lost poem "Crucifixión" is added to section 7, where it may well belong. With this addition section 7 has 182 verses. The first poem of this group of three says nothing directly about the intensely personal preoccupations so evident in many of the preceding poems. It is all about New York, and its message is not hard to interpret. In it the poet contrasts the inhuman mechanization and commercialization of life in New York with the blood and passion of exploited living beings. Denouncing the exploiters and taking his stand with the exploited, he offers himself in the final verses as a sacrificial victim. In this way he renews the harshly critical vein of several of the earlier poems.

"Jewish Cemetery" is another extremely difficult poem. For the present we will have to be satisfied with the most tentative and rudimentary of interpretations. The setting fluctuates between a Jewish cemetery seen as a cemetery and as a ship. The maritime imagery evokes the historical dimensions of a Jewish fate so often marked by exile, persecution, and death. The poem begins and ends with fevers called *alegres* (joyful), which is to say, the agents of death are content in the abode of death. The children of Christ (the Christians) are pictured as either happy or in no way afflicted by the plight of the Jews. By contrast, the Jews are presented as suffering the anguish of the unrelenting presence of death. What hope they have is pinned to the heart of a dove, but they can only muster half a dove, which is too small a sacrifice to redeem them. The particular Jew who enters the cemetery sees it as a kind of harbor, its marble tombs being likened to little boats. But the boats offer no prospect of escape from grim destiny, and the Jew cuts off his hands in silent acceptance of his ineluctable fate.[14]

---

14. Professor Elliot S. Glass has written the most interesting interpretation of this poem that I have seen. It is called "El cementerio judío: García Lorca's Historical Vision of the Jew." At this writing it remains unpublished. I quote a few sentences to give a general idea of its contents: "The poem, as shocking as it is accurate, depicts the Jews on board ships journeying to their bloody death. Unaware of their destiny or unwilling to acknowledge it, they are transported by the children of Christ who, when they are not rowing (actively participating) are sleeping (passively condoning). Stripped of all the appurtenances of civilization— materially and spiritually—the Jews prefer to preserve their own dignity and die by their own hand. . . . The result is a poignant indictment of Christianity" (p. 4 of Glass's typescript).

"Crucifixion" is about the (at least provisional) reconciliation of love and death. Against a backdrop of allusions to the Crucifixion of Christ, the poem expresses the cruel abuse of male and female love in a hostile world. Despite the attacks of the moon and the pharisees (social constraints?), both kinds of love seem to be saved as the world casts off trembling rivers of moths (destructive agents).[15]

Section 8, called simply "Dos odas," contains two poems totaling 211 verses. The first ode, "Grito hacia Roma," proclaims that disasters will descend upon the capital of Western Christendom, in part because the activities of the Church are of no avail in a world of violence and injustice. The degraded and suffering multitudes will cry out their anger and despair until the cities tremble and Earth's will is done, which yields its fruits for all. The dominant theme of the second poem, "Oda a Walt Whitman," is love. While its setting is New York (harshly criticized in now familiar ways), its meaning is not restricted to that city. Almost all kinds of love can be respected, including a certain kind of homosexual love represented by a Walt Whitman conceived as a noble and virile lover of men. Only the corrupt fairies of the cities are condemned: they are depicted as purveyors of death and corruption, enemies of joyful love. Like the first poem of this section, "Ode to Walt Whitman" ends with the wish that Earth's will be done, expressed in this case by a black child proclaiming to the wealthy whites the advent of the kingdom of wheat, which may well be the wheat of the Eucharist.

Section 9 is titled "Huida de Nueva York: Dos valses hacia la civilización," which amounts to eighty-eight verses. The first poem is "Pequeño vals vienés." In it the poet declares in his own first person his love for a "thou" of unspecified sex. Anything but gay, the waltz is full of the emotions and trappings of death. The second piece is "Vals en las ramas." More than the first, it appears on the surface to possess the charm of the rhythmical nonsense often found in children's poetry. A deeper look reveals the poet weeping over his wounds; what seemed like a gay dance is really a lullaby to fleshless bones. If the flight from New York is to some degree a movement from barbarism to civilization, it offers no escape from the uncertainties of love and the certainty of death.

Section 10, "El poeta llega a la Habana," contains only one poem of thirty-

---

15. Marcilly does not believe that the moths are meant to be taken negatively. For him they are another example of Lorca's love for the least of nature's creatures. I consider his interpretation implausible because of the usually violent connotations of the verb *arrojar*. See his "Notes pour l'Étude de la Pensée Religieuse de F. García Lorca: Crucifixión," *Bulletin Hispanique* 64 bis (1962): 521–24.

five verses, "Son de negros en Cuba." Its refrain, "I'll go to Santiago," repeated eighteen times, gives the poem a strong forward thrust appropriate to the flight from New York, which started with Viennese waltzes and now ends with a Cuban dance rhythm. Superficially gay and full of tropical elements (palm trees, cane fields, maracas, etc.), it moves with a typical ebb and flow of yearning and mortal despair: "*¡Oh curva de suspiro y barro!*" ("Oh curve of sigh and clay!"), p. 531.

Recent editions of the *Obras completas* (Aguilar) have added to *Poeta en Nueva York* two poems that do not appear in the first editions of the collection: "Pequeño poema infinito" and "La luna pudo detenerse al fin." It is not known where Lorca intended to fit these two poems into his book. I have already commented briefly on the second one under the title of "Crucifixión," which is the title the poet gave it. The comments were placed at the end of section 7, mostly because Ben Belitt and Angel del Río have suggested that it belongs there and I have found no evidence to justify a different location.[16] So far as I know, a logical place for "Pequeño poema infinito" has not been proposed.[17] This poem combines three of the capital themes of the book: religion, love, and death. It opens like this:

Equivocar el camino
es llegar a la nieve
y llegar a la nieve
es pacer durante veinte siglos las hierbas de los cementerios.   (p. 531)

> To mistake the way
> is to reach the snow
> and to reach the snow
> is to graze for twenty centuries the grass of the cemeteries.

The "way" is surely the one Christ said He was; to mistake the way is to arrive at death, so the horses of love graze for twenty centuries (i.e., since the death of Christ) on the fodder of death. The rest of the poem deals largely with the anguishing commerce between love and death. The poem is called infinite, because the love-death cycle seems without end.

16. See del Río's Introduction, p. xxiv.
17. Eisenberg writes: "Above all, it is evident that "Pequeño poema infinito" does not belong to *Poeta*, nor did it ever belong to this work . . . (*Poeta en Nueva York . . .*, p. 123). To me it does not seem so evident, but in any case, it was written in New York and dated 10 January 1930. Its style and contents are consistent with the other New York poems.

Aside from the poems that are supposed to be lost, there exist others that seem to belong to the canon of *Poeta en Nueva York*. One is called "Infancia y muerte" and is dated in New York on 7 October 1929. It was first published in 1975 by Martínez Nadal, who has written that Lorca decided not to include it in his new book.[18] Another poem very much in the style of the New York poems is "Tierra y luna," dated in Spain in 1935, but nothing is known of the poet's intentions with regard to this poem; prudence seems to dictate that it and a few others of similar uncertainty be left aside for now.

One of the reasons for undertaking the rough inventory just concluded was to discover the main themes of *Poeta en Nueva York* and to discover to what extent the poet had succeeded in organizing them in some meaningful way. The Introduction pointed to some reasons for believing that he intended to do so, but, as we know, he did not live to see his book in print. This circumstance should be remembered as we search for significance in the structure of *Poeta en Nueva York.*

Perhaps the most sensible overall commentary on the book is still the one that del Río published in 1955 as the Introduction to Ben Belitt's translation of the New York poems. As Lorca's friend and even a witness to the genesis of some parts of the book, del Río was aware of the problematical character of its organization: "The book was created very slowly and never assumed a final form satisfactory to the author, since he left it unpublished" (p. xvii). But despite the textual blemishes and uncertainties, del Río concluded: "As the book has finally reached us, it has a clear organization externally, as well as an inner sequence of the moods and impulses of the poet" (p. xviii). This conclusion sounds plausible to the present writer. It is his guess that had Lorca lived to supervise the publication of his New York book, he might have found appropriate places into which to fit the unincluded poems generally thought to belong to the New York canon, but it is doubtful that they would have served to overturn the existing organization. If this is only an educated guess, it is at least the only prudent principle on which to base a study. It would be capricious to assume anything else unless new indications by the poet himself should come to light.

In his account of the existing organization of *Poeta en Nueva York*, Professor del Río found that the ten sections of the book correspond to five alternate moments of spiritual experience, which he describes very briefly. These descriptions rest in part on analysis of the thematic structure of the book and in part on what del Río knew of the moods, activities, and movements of the

18. See Federico García Lorca: Autógrafos I, p. xxxv.

poet. They are not very detailed nor calculated to make the structure itself yield added significance to the book.

Beginning where del Río left off, Richard Saez does try to find additional meaning in the structure. Here is how he describes his undertaking: "Professor Angel del Río describes Lorca's arrival in New York, his temporary refuge in Newburg, Vermont [sic], his return to the city, and his final departure. These are described in this essay allegorically as Lorca's descent (as quester) into the abysmal Waste Land, his defeat and temporary flight, and his return and eventual triumph over the Waste Land Monsters." [19] Although it contains some provocative insights into the meaning of *Poeta en Nueva York*, Saez's essay does not succeed in creating a convincing interpretation on the pattern outlined above.[20]

In her recent study of *Poeta en Nueva York* Betty Jean Craige finds an overall meaning in the book. She expresses it in a variety of ways that can at least be suggested by two or three quotations. The subtitle of her book is "The Fall into Consciousness," so *Poeta en Nueva York* can be seen as a modern reenactment of the Biblical Fall: "The myth of the Fall expresses both the state of man's alienation from God and nature, resulting from consciousness, and the state of modern civilization's alienation from any spiritually unifying reality which might have held society together as a community" (p. 2). But it is a recovery as well as a fall: "Thus *Poet in New York* is the symbolization of Lorca's experience of depression and isolation in a foreign reality he apprehends as a hostile chaos. It is therefore the account of a psychic journey from alienation and disorientation toward reintegration into the natural world (p. 2). And the reintegration is furthered by sacrifice: "Thus *Poet in New York* may be viewed as a soul's symbolic journey from Adam to Christ, with Adam becoming Christ through sacrifice" (p. 85). I don't believe these ideas can be fully and convincingly documented in Lorca's book, but they are worth thinking about.[21]

19. See his "The Ritual Sacrifice in Lorca's *Poet in New York*," in *Lorca: A Collection of Critical Essays*, ed. Manuel Durán (Englewood Cliffs, N.J.: Prentice-Hall, 1962), pp. 108–9.

20. Saez's essay fails, I believe, because he carries supposed analogies with Eliot's *The Waste Land* beyond what the texts will sustain, because he ignores sizable portions of *Poeta en Nueva York*, and because he relies too heavily on Belitt's translation, which often betrays the sense of Lorca's verse.

21. Even if Ms. Craige's interpretation were judged to be correct as far as it goes, it would still fail to account for much that is undeniably important. She discusses only a little over half of the poems in the books and she completely ignores the role in them of the heavy psychic burden that was not born in New York but carried there from Spain.

So far as I know, there are no other attempts to analyze in detail the significant structure of the book.[22]

As we try once more to reach a better understanding of the thematic structure of the book, we should remember that the poet thought about it as a way of putting his poetic world in contact with the poetic world of New York. With this in mind, we may say that "Poems of Solitude at Columbia University," while implying a New York setting for the first poem, is otherwise all about the poetic world of Lorca. Its major themes are love, death, lost innocence, lost friendship, and thwarted fulfillment. Love and death are perennial themes, which often coalesce into a single love-death theme. We may call the love introduced in section 1 "ambiguous love," whose label might be changed to "forbidden love" when it is perceived as in conflict with social norms. A striking aspect of the death theme in this first section is that it takes the form of anticipating the poet's own death, an anticipation that haunts the rest of the book. The poet senses that he must live his life in the unresolved tension of antithetical forces, and these will be illustrated on many levels.

Section 2 introduces the blacks. In the first poem their nature is described as natural, spontaneous, and sensual. The second poem describes the plight of a people with such a nature in the antithetical culture of New York. With this poem the characterization and indictment of the metropolis is initiated. The central theme of the last poem of this section is the troubled spirit of a poet who has lost his religious faith. By the end of section 2 all the major themes of the book have been introduced. The other eight sections combine and elaborate them in such a way as to cause the poet's sense of the two worlds to reinforce each other.

Section 3 carries the reader into the chaotic world of "Streets and Dreams." The streets are New York's, the dreams are the poet's. Together they express the confusion and suffering of both, ever tormented by the blind forces of love and death.

Section 4 takes the reader out of New York into the peaceful setting of rural Vermont. In this setting the poet recalls a time before he knew "the bitter juices" of frustrated love. He cries out for freedom to love in his own

22. Twenty years ago Gustavo Correa published a brief but perceptive overview of *Poeta en Nueva York* titled "Significado de 'Poeta en Nueva York' de Federico García Lorca," *Cuadernos Americanos* 18 (1959): 224–33. Although this essay is worth reading, I don't quote it in the text, because I don't consider correct much of what is most original in it, namely, his discussion of archetypal symbols. The moon, for example, is presented as a "fecund and beneficial presence" reduced to impotence in the hostile world of New York (p. 230). I think it is now well established that in Lorca's works the moon is usually a negative element.

human way. But, as in the opening poem of the book, he senses his own doom *"allí donde flota mi cuerpo entre los equilibrios contrarios"* ("there where my body floats between balanced opposites"), p. 499. The second poem envisions the possible achievement of the amorous freedom called for in the first.

Still in a rural setting, section 5 contains three poems about the unrelenting and unmotivated presence of death. In "Vaca" the cow is presented as a kind of sacrificial victim, thus preparing the way for subsequent references to the cow, particularly in "New York: Oficina y denuncia" and in "Crucifixión."

If section 4 is mostly about love and section 5 is mostly about death, section 6 combines the two themes. Death is the great destroyer of love, and yet it is death that lends value and urgency to love.

Section 7 brings the reader back to the inhuman mechanization and commercialization of the great city. In it the poet's own death assumes a new form, that of a sacrificial victim. "Cementerio judío" represents the grim fate of the Jews, whose hope for survival rests on (the sacrifice of?) a dove, which does not seem to be sufficient. "Crucifixión" continues the theme of sacrifice and holds out the possibility of the reconciliation of love and death.

Section 8, in its first poem, extends the denunciation of New York to the whole Western world. It prophesies that disasters will befall Rome, because the role of the Church has been of so little avail in a world of unremitting violence and injustice, thus carrying the poet's abandonment of the Church to a wider arena. The second poem exalts Walt Whitman and all kinds of love except that of the corrupt fairies, thus bringing to open affirmation a love that began as ambiguous and had remained forbidden. Both poems end with the hope that some day Earth's will may be done, thus obliquely recalling that the efficacy of Heaven's will has already been discounted. The second poem would have a black child announce to the wealthy whites the coming kingdom of the spikes of grain, thus foreshadowing a resolution of the plight of the blacks and other oppressed peoples.

Sections 9 and 10 express the flight from New York and the arrival in Havana. They are given the form of dances, thus reducing the anguish of the nightmare rhythms of New York. Nevertheless, the flight from barbarism to civilization offers no relief from the sorrow of fleeting love and irredeemable death.

4

The poet's vision of New York

The poets of Lorca's generation (often called the Generation of 1927) have been characterized as cerebral artists devoted to a playful art, formally demanding, but not much given to expressing the deeper feelings of the human heart. If there is any truth to this characterization, it is more applicable to the early works of that generation than to their mature works; that is to say, their poetry evolves toward an intensely human art, even to an art that is in some cases socially and politically revolutionary.[1] Lorca's poetry was never as cold

A shorter version of this chapter appeared in Spanish in an essay titled "Nueva York y la conciencia social de Federico García Lorca," *Revista Hispánica Moderna*, 36 (1970–71): 32–40.

1. For a valuable personal account of this generation, see Dámaso Alonso, *Poetas españoles contemporáneos* (Madrid, 1952), pp. 167–92. The evolution alluded to above can be clearly seen in the poetry of Dámaso Alonso himself, whose confirming words are these: "Nothing do I now detest more than the sterile estheticism in which contemporary art has been floundering about for more than half a century. Today what interests me is only the heart of man: to express with my sorrow or with my hope the longing or the anguish of the eternal heart of man" (p. 178).

and intellectual as the first fruits of some of the other poets of his generation, but it too underwent a similar evolution and his stay in New York seems to have been a milestone in that evolution.

The purpose of this chapter is to examine what Lorca called the poetic world of New York. In our overview of *Poeta en Nueva York*, we saw some of the essential elements of the poet's vision of New York, but we will look at them now more fully and with some reference to the poet's heightened awareness of social injustice.

In a letter of early June 1929 Federico announced to his friend Carlos Morla Lynch his intention of spending six or seven months in America, adding: "New York seems to me horrible, but that's exactly why I am going there" (p. 1673). Direct experience of New York confirmed this judgment enunciated prior to the visit.[2] Why did it seem horrible? Before seeking specific answers to this question, it may be useful to gather some preliminary impressions of the quality of the poet's vision of New York by noting some surprising word frequencies.[3] One might expect to find an abundance of technical and industrial vocabulary, but, although it is represented in some of the poems, it does not show any conspicuous frequency. Contrary to what might be expected, animal vocabulary is abundant. In chapter 2 we observed that *caballo* is used in *Poeta en Nueva York* an amazing two dozen times. Another animal mentioned with surprising frequency is *vaca*. In all of Lorca's poetry the cow is mentioned seventeen times, fifteen of which occur in the New York poems! And there are a few exotic animals found in these poems only. Four examples are: *caimán* (alligator), *cobra* (cobra), *iguana* (iguana), and *tiburón* (shark). Without exhausting the list of fauna in *Poeta en Nueva York* it is probably safe to offer at least these generalizations about their function: Some of them are present to play now-familiar symbolic roles; some are present to convey such notions as evil or cruelty or the ultimate retribution that Nature will visit upon the unfeeling metropolis; sometimes the mere naming of them serves to suggest how much of Nature's realm is absent from the city.

Actually, absence or emptiness may be regarded as an important theme. The city with all its teeming multitudes is typically perceived as full of emptiness. A key word in this connection is *hueco* (empty place, void) used fifteen times in these poems out of a total occurrence of sixteen in Lorca's poetry.[4]

2. By exception, in a second letter to Morla Lynch, Lorca says of New York that "it is a city of unsuspected gaiety" (p. 1674).

3. Derived from Alice M. Pollin's *A Concordance to the Plays and Poems of Federico García Lorca* (Ithaca, N.Y., and London: Cornell University Press, 1975).

4. Martínez Nadal has called attention to the significance of *hueco* in Lorca's writings. See his *El público . . .*, pp. 113–15.

Other oft-repeated words belonging to the same category of ideas are: *vacío* (empty), *huella* (trace, track), which is the mark left by what is no longer present, and the adjective *solo* (alone, lonely). Even the much-used word *guante* (glove) might be added to this list, since it is usually present empty of the human hand it was meant to protect or adorn.

The murderous violence and the anguish which are part of the poet's vision of New York are also expressed by the obsessive frequency of certain key words. For example, *asesinar* and its derivatives are employed ten times in the New York poems out of a total of twelve in all of the poetry. A word used exclusively in these poems is *devorar* (devour) and its derivatives (nine times). Finally, *angustia* (anguish) is used only eleven times in all of Lorca's poetry, nine of which belong to the New York poems. These few examples by no means exhaust the list of significant high-frequency words, but too many lexical statistics would become tedious.

One of the unpleasant aspects of New York that impressed the poet is filth of one kind or another. It is evoked by such words as *cieno* (slime), *fango* (mire), *podrido* (putrid):

La aurora de Nueva York tiene
cuatro columnas de cieno
y un huracán de negras palomas
que chapotean las aguas podridas.   ("La aurora," p. 497)

    Dawn in New York has
    four columns of slime
    and a hurricane of black pigeons
    that splash about in the putrid waters.

In a figurative sense the filth is associated with money: "*Son los vivísimos hormigueros y las monedas en el fango*" ("Navidad en el Hudson," p. 491). "It's the liveliest anthills and the coins in the mire." And with death:

Nueva York de cieno,
Neueva York de alambre y de muerte.   ("Oda a Walt Whitman," p. 523)

    New York of slime.
    New York of wire and death.

In spite of the poet's announced intention not to write an external description of New York, he recalls repeatedly certain architectural features, particularly its *aristas* (the sharp exterior edges or angles called "arris"), *esquinas* (corners), *escaleras* (stairs, fire escapes), and *ventanas* (windows). Something of what these features represented for Lorca is revealed in this fragment of a 1933 interview:

> Extrahuman architecture and furious rhythm, geometry and anguish. Nevertheless, there is no joy despite the rhythm. Man and machine live the servitude of the moment. The arris rise to the sky with no will to cloud or glory. . . . Armies of windows where not a single person has time to look at a cloud or converse with one of the delicate breezes which the sea stubbornly sends without ever receiving a reply . . ." (p. 1713).

The sad thing about these architectural features is that they are perceived to serve no human end. The numberless *escaleras,* for example: seldom is there reference to their function and when there is it tends to be sinister:

Nos caemos por las escaleras para comer la tierra húmeda
o subimos al filo de la nieve con el coro de las dalias muertas.

("Ciudad sin sueño," p. 493)

> We fall down the stairs to eat the damp earth or
> we climb to the edge of the snow with the chorus of dead dahlias.

For the most part, they are only a component of the cityscape: *"el paisaje de las escaleras"* ("the landscape of the fire escapes"), p. 486. The dawn seeks a human sense among the sharp angles of the geometric city but in vain:

La aurora de Nueva York gime
por las inmensas escaleras
buscando entre las aristas
nardos de angustia dibujada.

("La aurora," p. 497)

> Dawn in New York moans
> up and down the immense fire escapes
> seeking among the arris
> nards of anguish designed.

The numberless windows also are lacking in human meaning: perhaps that is why they appear vaguely menacing. Here are two examples from "Danza de la muerte": *"el cielo tendrá que huir ante el tumulto de las ventanas"* (p. 485); "the sky will have to flee before the tumult of the windows"; and *"Enjambres de ventanas acribillaban un muslo de la noche"* (p. 486); "Swarms of windows riddled a thigh of the night." In spite of an abundance that prompts the poet to see them as tumults, swarms, and armies, the windows do not seem to put man in contact with Nature.

New York not only lives apart from Nature, it demands of her a monstrous sacrifice of animal life:

Todos los días se matan en Nueva York
cuatro millones de patos,
cinco millones de cerdos,
dos mil palomas para el gusto de los agonizantes,
un millón de vacas,
un millón de corderos
y dos millones de gallos ...   ("Nueva York: Oficina y denuncia," pp. 515–16)

    Every day in New York they kill
    four million ducks,
    five million pigs,
    two thousand pigeons for the pleasure of the dying,
    a million cows,
    a million lambs,
    and two million roosters ...

The most distressing aspect of this Gargantuan appetite for animal flesh is the vast commercialization it entails:

Más vale sollozar afilando la navaja
o asesinar a los perros
en las alucinantes cacerías,
que resistir en la madrugada
los interminables trenes de leche,
los interminables trenes de sangre
y los trenes de rosas maniatadas
por los comerciantes de perfumes.   (ibid., p. 516)

    Better to sob sharpening the razor
    or to murder the dogs
    in the hallucinatory hunts,
    than to endure at dawn
    the endless trains of milk,
    the endless trains of blood
    and the trains of roses shackled
    by the dealers in perfumes.

The city may foment cruelty:

los niños machacaban pequeñas ardillas
con un rubor de frenesí manchado.   ("Oda al rey de Harlem," p. 478)

> the children pounded little squirrels
> with a flush of tainted frenzy.

Or, at least, an incapacity to appreciate the value of even the humblest of creatures:

Hay un mundo de ríos quebrados
y distancias inasibles
en la patita de ese gato
quebrada por el automóvil.   ("New York: Oficina y denuncia," p. 517)

> There is a world of broken rivers
> and of unattainable distances
> in that cat's little paw
> broken by the automobile.

For Lorca, New York was the city of numbers, of multiplications, of collectivities, especially of anonymous human collectivities. Individuals are seldom mentioned. Human types are presented almost always in the plural: children, blacks, girls, mulattoes, sailors, Jewesses, soldiers, whores, dancers, fairies, builders, unemployed workers, peoples. They are so anonymous that they may show up as landscapes. The reader has already seen two titles of poems that illustrate this point: "Landscape of the Vomiting Multitude" and "Landscape of the Urinating Multitude." At times they are so vacuous that they appear to be a congregation of clothes: "¡Ay, Harlem, amenazada por un gentío de trajes sin cabeza!" ("Oh, Harlem, threatened by a throng of suits without heads!"), p. 482. Or:

Un traje abandonado pesa tanto en los hombros
que muchas veces el cielo los agrupa en ásperas manadas.
                    ("Panorama ciego de Nueva York," p. 495)

> A cast-off suit weighs so much on the shoulders
> that heaven often gathers them in sullen herds.

Their work is inhuman:

No hay más que un millón de herreros
forjando cadenas para los niños que han de venir.
No hay más que un millón de carpinteros
que hacen ataúdes sin cruz.
No hay más que un gentío de lamentos
que se abren las ropas en espera de la bala.

("Grito hacia Roma," pp. 520–21)

> There are only a million blacksmiths
> forging chains for the children yet to come.
> There are only a million carpenters
> who make coffins without crosses.
> There is only a legion of laments
> undoing their clothing to await the bullet.

And:

Saben que van al cieno de números y leyes,
a los juegos sin arte, a sudores sin fruto.

("La aurora," p. 497)

> They know that they are going to the slime of numbers and laws,
> to games without art, to sweat without fruit.

Their movements are awkward and without hope:

No hay remedio para el gemido del velero japonés,
ni para estas gentes ocultas que tropiezan con las esquinas.

("Paisaje de la multitud que orina," p. 490)

> There is no hope for the moan from the Japanese sailing ship,
> nor for these hidden people who stumble against the corners.

They can be seen as hapless insomniacs:

Por los barrios hay gentes que vacilan insomnes
como recien salidas de un naufragio de sangre.

("La aurora," p. 497)

> In the slums there are sleepless people who stagger
> as though just delivered from a shipwreck of blood.

For them there are no fiestas unless it be *"la última fiesta de los taladros"* ("the final feast of the wormholes"), p. 516.

Among the human groups of keenest interest to the poet were the blacks. In an already-quoted interview, he explained: "I wanted to make the poem of the black race in North America and to underline the suffering they experience in being black in a contrary world; slaves of all the inventions of the white man and of all his machines . . ." (pp. 1714–15). The poems dedicated to the blacks underscore both their anger and their suffering. Their anger rages partly because it has no outlet, although more than once it is suggested that it will find an outlet in the coming day of retribution:

La sangre no tiene puertas en vuestra noche boca arriba.
No hay rubor. Sangre furiosa por debajo de las pieles,
viva en la espina del puñal y en el pecho de los paisajes,
bajo las pinzas y las retamas de la celeste luna de cáncer.

("Oda al rey de Harlem," p. 480)

Blood has no gateways in your over-turned night.
There is no flush. Blood rages under the skins,
alive on the thorn of the dagger and in the heart of the landscapes,
under the pincers and furze of Cancer's celestial moon.

There is anguish beyond words:

¡Ay Harlem! ¡Ay Harlem! ¡Ay Harlem!
¡No hay angustia comparable a tus ojos oprimidos,
a tu sangre estremecida dentro del eclipse oscuro,
a tu violencia granate sordomuda en la penumbra,
a tu gran rey prisionero con un traje de conserje.   (ibid., p. 479)

Oh Harlem! Oh Harlem! Oh Harlem!
There is no anguish comparable to your oppressed eyes,
to your blood trembling in dark eclipse,
to your garnet violence deaf and dumb in the shadows,
to your great king prisoner in a janitor's suit.

The grief is caused in part by the servility so often demanded of them:

Es por el silencio sapientísimo
cuando los camereros y los cocineros y los que limpian con sus lenguas
las heridas de los millonarios
buscan al rey por las calles o en los ángulos del salitre.   (ibid., p. 481)

It's the wisest silence
when the waiters and cooks and those who clean with their tongues
the wounds of the millionaires
look for the king in the streets or on the corners of saltpeter.

For Lorca, the black is "close to pure human nature and to the other nature" (p. 1699). Part of the black's suffering, therefore, can be attributed to his living in a denaturalized and mechanical city while he feels himself so drawn to the natural and the spontaneous:

Aman el azul desierto,
las vacilantes expresiones bovinas,
la mentirosa luna de los polos,
la danza curva del agua en la orilla.

("Norma y paraíso de los negros," p. 477)

They love the desert blue,
the hesitant bovine expressions,
the deceitful moon of the poles,
the curving dance of the water on the shore.

One of the things that wounded the sensibilities of the poet in New York was Wall Street with all the superhuman riches and power it seemed to represent. In 1933 he remembered it thus: "Impressive for its coldness and its cruelty. Gold flows there in rivers from all parts of the earth, and death arrives with it" (p. 1715). And that is the way he portrayed it in *Poeta en Nueva York*. Money corrupts everything: "*Las muchachas americanas llevaban niños y monedas en el vientre*" ("American girls carried children and coins in their bellies"), "Oda al rey de Harlem," p. 479. Wall Street is seen as a kind of columbarium which attracts gold and death:

No es extraño para la danza
este columbario que pone los ojos amarillos.
De la esfinge a la caja de caudales hay un hilo tenso
que atraviesa el corazón de todos los niños pobres.

("Danza de la muerte," p. 485)

This columbarium turning eyes yellow
is not strange for the dance.
From the sphinx to the bank vault there is a taut wire
that transfixes the hearts of all poor children.

The poet lays special stress on the baneful influence of money on the fate of abandoned children:

A veces las monedas en enjambres furiosos
taladran y devoran abandonados niños.   ("La aurora," p. 497)

    Sometimes coins in furious swarms
    pierce and devour abandoned children.

So baneful does the poet feel the influence of Wall Street to be that it seems to him an appropriate setting in which to concentrate some of his bitterest reactions to his American experience:

No es extraño este sitio para la danza, yo lo digo.
El mascarón bailará entre columnas de sangre y de números,
entre huracanes de oro y gemidos de obreros parados
que aullarán, noche oscura, por tu tiempo sin luces,
¡oh salvaje Norteamérica! ¡Oh impúdica! ¡Oh salvaje!,
tendida en la frontera de la nieve!   ("Danza de la muerte," p. 486)

    This is not a strange place for the dance, I tell you so.
    The mask will dance among the columns of blood and of numbers,
    among hurricanes of gold and groans of jobless workers
    who will howl in the dark night of your benighted time,
    Oh savage North America! Oh shameless! Oh savage America,
    stretched out on the frontier of snow!

It sometimes seems as though the imagination of the poet converted New York into a vast stage on which to exhibit the ugliest face of the contemporary world, its growing dehumanization and injustice. An essential part of *Poeta en Nueva York* is in one form or another a protest against the monstrous metropolis. The poet denounces its cruelty and indifference:

Yo denuncio a toda la gente
que ignora la otra mitad,
la mitad irredimible
que levanta sus montes de cemento
donde laten los corazones
de los animalitos que se olvidan
y donde caeremos todos
en la última fiesta de los taladros.   ("New York: Oficina y denuncia," p. 516)

> I denounce all the people
> who are unaware of the other half,
> the irredeemable half
> that raises its mountains of cement
> where beat the hearts
> of the little animals now forgotten
> and where we shall all fall
> at the final feast of the wormholes.

In other verses the denunciation is directed at the indifferent, impersonal character of the city:

> Yo denuncio la conjura
> de estas desiertas oficinas
> que no radian las agonías
> que borran los programas de las selvas.   (ibid., 517)

> I denounce the conspiracy
> of these deserted offices
> that do not broadcast the death agonies
> that erase the programs of the forests.

Repeatedly the poet prophesies that Nature will avenge herself on a city from which she has for so many years been exiled. His counsel to the blacks is:

> Aguardad bajo la sombra vegetal de vuestro rey
> a que cicutas y cardos y ortigas turben postreras azoteas.
>   ("Oda al rey de Harlem," p. 482)

> Wait beneath the vegetable shadow of your king
> for poison hemlock, thistles and nettles to alarm the furthermost rooftops.

He announces the advent of revolution, imagining two variations of the final collapse of the metropolis:

> Que ya las cobras silbarán por los últimos pisos,
> que ya las ortigas estremecerán patios y terrazas,
> que ya la Bolsa será una pirámide de musgo,
> que ya vendrán lianas después de los fusiles
> y muy pronto, muy pronto, muy pronto.
> ¡Ay, Wall Street!   ("Danza de la muerte," p. 487)

> For soon cobras will hiss on topmost floors,
> soon nettles will shake patios and terraces,

soon the Stock Market will be a pyramid of moss,
soon jungle vines will follow the rifles
and very soon, very soon, very soon.
Oh, Wall Street!

The repeated references to obnoxious plants are reminiscent of Isaiah's prophecy of the destruction of Edom and Israel: "Thorns shall sprout in its palaces;/ nettles and briars shall cover its walled towns" (34.13).

In the second version of the collapse of the city, it is the protest of the abused masses that will shake the foundations:

Mientras tanto, mientras tanto, ¡ay! mientras tanto,
los negros que sacan las escupideras,
los muchachos que tiemblan bajo el terror pálido de los directores,
las mujeres ahogadas en aceites minerales,
la muchedumbre de martillo, de violín o de nube,
ha de gritar aunque le estrellen los sesos en el muro,
ha de gritar frente a las cúpulas,
ha de gritar loca de fuego,
ha de gritar loca de nieve,
ha de gritar con la cabeza llena de excremento,
ha de gritar como todas las noches juntas,
ha de gritar con voz tan desgarrada
hasta que las ciudades tiemblen como niñas
y rompan las prisiones de aceite y la música . . .

("Grito hacia Roma," p. 522)

Meanwhile, meanwhile, oh, meanwhile,
the blacks who set out the cuspidors,
the boys who tremble under the pale terror of the schoolmasters,
the women drowning in mineral oil,
the crowd of the hammer, violin or cloud,
will cry out even though their brains are dashed against the wall,
will cry out facing the cupolas,
will cry out mad with fire,
will cry out mad with snow,
will cry out with their heads full of excrement,
will cry out like all nights in one,
will cry out with a voice torn by anguish
until the cities tremble like little girls
and break the prisons of oil and the music . . .

The protest is launched in the name of elementary justice:

porque queremos el pan nuestro de cada día,
flor de aliso y perenne ternura desgranada,
porque queremos que se cumpla la voluntad de la Tierra
que da sus frutos para todos.   (ibid.)

> because we want our daily bread,
> alder flower and everlasting tenderness threshed,
> because we want Earth's will to be done,
> Earth that bears its fruits for all.

One cannot affirm that Lorca's New York residence first awoke in him a sense of social justice, because he had already expressed such a sense in his very first book. Here from that book are some pertinent lines about a Galician orphanage:

> This enormous squat entrance gate has seen passing through it interminable processions of human specters who entering uneasily have left there abandoned children. . . . I was deeply moved by this gate through which so many wretched ones have passed. . . . and it must know its mission and want to die of grief, because it is worm-eaten, dirty, rickety. Perhaps someday, feeling pity for the hungry children and for the grave social injustices, it will crash down on some city welfare committee, where there are so many frock coat bandits, and by squashing them make a beautiful omelet of the kind so badly needed in Spain. . . . (p. 1690)[5]

No other social protest of comparable vehemence can be found in Lorca's writings until his sojourn in New York, which, it should be remembered, was in the throes of the Great Depression. But from that time forward his concern for social justice was voiced again and again and was accompanied by a growing urge to communicate with the masses and to contribute with his art to their welfare. The statements that attest these concerns belong to the years 1932–36, when his New York impressions remained strong and he was becoming ever more aware of the conditions in Spain that were to lead to the Spanish Civil War. Even though it takes us beyond *Poeta en Nueva York*, it may be appropriate to conclude this chapter with a brief review of these statements.

The poet takes his stand with the poor: "In this world I am and always will be a partisan of those who have nothing and are denied even the peace of mind

5. Words first published in *Impresiones y paisajes* (Granada, 1918), pp. 248–49.

of having nothing" (p. 1766). Realizing the importance of socioeconomic problems, he refers in these terms to a new play: "The truth of the comedy is a religious and socio-economic problem. The world is held back by the hunger that destroys the peoples. So long as there is economic unbalance, the world doesn't think. . . . The day hunger disappears, there will occur in the world the greatest spiritual explosion Humanity has ever known. Man will never be able to imagine the joy that will burst forth the day of the Great Revolution. I am talking to you like a true socialist, am I not?" (p. 1812). As we have seen, there is a glimmer of that revolution in *Poeta en Nueva York*.

On more than one occasion Lorca said that his desire to reach the masses was one of the powerful motives that led him to write for the theater: "In our age, the poet must open his veins for the others. That's why, aside from the reasons I told you before, I have devoted myself to the theater, which allows us a more direct contact with the masses" (p. 1771).

Although calling himself "an ardent devotee of the theater of social action" (p. 150), there are days when the poet realizes the possible futility of his efforts. Even so, to continue to write for the theater may stand as a kind of protest: "But one must work, work. Work and help him who deserves it. Work even though one sometimes thinks he makes a useless effort. Work as a form of protest. Because one's impulse would be to shout every day on waking to a world full of injustice and destitution of all kinds: I protest! I protest! I protest!" (p. 1771).

The poet expresses his solidarity with his people: "In this dramatic moment of the world [1936], the artist must weep and laugh with his people. One must lay down the bouquet of lilies and enter the mire up to his waist to help those that seek the lilies" (p. 1814). He understands the need for sacrifice: "We—I refer to men who count intellectually, who were brought up in the average surroundings of the classes that we might call well-off—are called to sacrifice. Let us accept the call" (p. 1766). The poet's will to sacrifice was first expressed in one of his New York poems:

y me ofrezco a ser comido
por las vacas estrujadas
cuando sus gritos llenan el valle
donde el Hudson se emborracha de aceite.

("New York: Oficina y denuncia," p. 517)

    and I offer myself to be
    eaten by the crushed cows
    when their cries fill the valley
    where the Hudson gets drunk on oil.

5

Tormented love

Love in all its forms is one of the two great themes in Lorca's poetry, the other being death. Just how all-embracing his vision of love is can be appreciated in the following quotation from the prologue to his first play:

> What reason do you have to look down on the least of Nature? So long as you do not deeply love the stone and the worm, you will not enter the Kingdom of God. The old sylph also said to the poet: "Very soon the kingdom of the animals and the plants will arrive; man forgets his creator, and the animal and the plant are very close to His light; poet, say to men that love is born with the same intensity on all planes of life; the leaf cradled by the breeze has the same rhythm as the distant star; that the same words said by the fountain in the shadows are said in the same tone by the sea; tell man to be humble; in Nature everything is equal!" (p. 670)

One senses that the love mentioned in these youthful outpourings is regarded as wholly attractive and noble, but one soon learns that the poet conceives of love in many other ways. In his first book, he asserts that all Nature yearns for sexual union;[1] in an early poem he calls sexual love a carnal hell (p. 291); love may distribute crowns of joy (p. 525); more often it evokes less attractive notions: anguish (p. 565), madness (p. 640), a sharp and wounding edge (p. 492), and a living death (p. 639).

Although the poet expresses love and understanding of the least of God's creatures, it is of course human love that looms the largest in his poetry. In all the published poems up to and including those in the *Romancero gitano*, the object of love (usually erotic desire) is most often woman, clearly identified by allusions to her feminine form. Most of the identifying words are unambiguous in their contexts: *pechos* (breasts), *senos* (breasts), *vientre* (belly-womb), *trenzas* (braids), for example. *Muslos* (thighs), although equally applicable to men, is also much used in contexts that permit no doubt that the thighs are feminine. In *Poeta en Nueva York*, a remarkable change occurs: the clearly recognizable female form all but disappears. As in earlier poems, there are powerfully erotic passages. In "Tu infancia en Menton," for example:

Allí, león, allí furia del cielo,
te dejaré pacer en mis mejillas;   (p. 476)

> There, lion, there heaven's fury,
> I'll let you graze on my cheeks.

But in the entire poem from which these verses are taken there is not one unambiguous anatomical reference. A part of the body often named in this and other similar poems is *cintura* (waist), but there is no reliable way of telling whose waist it is. This style of ambiguity is characteristic of all the love poems in *Poeta en Nueva York*, and is surely deliberate. It is one of the clues that lead the attentive reader to conclude that the dominant aspect of love expressed in the New York poems is that of love between men.[2] Before we examine the other clues, it must be noted that procreative love is also present and should be looked at first.

Most of the references to the love that produces offspring appear in passages

1. See Lorca's *Impresiones y paisajes*, p. 226.

2. No one emphasizes as much as Jean-Louis Schonberg the importance in *Poeta en Nueva York* of the theme of homosexual love. He thinks he has found the key to its full interpretation in *The Thousand and One Nights* and in Sigmund Freud's *Introduction to Psychoanalysis*. The theme is indeed a major one, but Schonberg pushes it to ridiculous extremes. The curious reader may see his *À la recherche de Lorca* (Neuchâtel: la Baconnière, 1966), pp. 232–52.

of futility and despair. In "Navidad en el Hudson" the poet evokes a lonely world in a lonely sky where death prevails. The verses that follow are found in the second half of the poem:

Y estoy con las manos vacías en el rumor de la desembocadura.
No importa que cada minuto
un niño nuevo agite sus ramitos de venas,
ni que el parto de la víbora, desatado bajo las ramas,
calme la sed de sangre de los que miran el desnudo.
Lo que importa es esto: hueco. Mundo solo. Desembocadura.   (p. 492)

    And I am empty-handed in the murmur of the rivermouth.
    It doesn't matter that each minute
    a new child may agitate the tiny branches of his veins,
    nor that the viper's delivery, released under the branches,
    may calm the blood-thirst of those who gaze upon the nude.
    What matters is this: empty space. Lonely world. Rivermouth.

The birth of new life does not appear to alter the essential emptiness of the world. In the next poem, "Ciudad sin sueño," a passage of analogous import occurs in a context expressing the mortal destiny of man:

Pero no hay olvido ni sueño:
carne viva. Los besos atan las bocas
en una maraña de venas recientes
y al que le duele su dolor le dolerá sin descanso
y el que teme la muerte la llevará sobre sus hombros.   (p. 493)

    But there is no oblivion or dream:
    living flesh. Kisses tie mouths
    in a tangle of recent veins
    and he whose sorrow grieves him will grieve without rest
    and he who fears death will carry it on his shoulders.

Again, new life affords no shield against the chill prospect of death.

Before attempting to relate these two passages to the main theme of this chapter and with the aim of reassuring ourselves that the attitude expressed is an essential one, let us look again at four more verses from a later poem called "Gacela de la huida":

> No hay noche que, al dar un beso,
> no sienta la sonrisa de las gentes sin rostro,
> ni hay nadie que, al tocar un recién nacido,
> olvide las inmóviles calaveras de caballo.   (p. 565)

>> There is no night that, on giving a kiss,
>> I don't sense the smile of the faceless people,
>> nor is there anyone who, on touching a new-born child,
>> forgets the motionless horse skulls.

Procreation, then, is part of a futile cycle leading irrevocably to death. In Lorca's poetic world this idea is widespread and eventually becomes a kind of justification of homosexual love, by which new life is not engendered merely to satisfy the appetite of death. An allusion to this justification is present in the "Oda a Walt Whitman":

> Porque es justo que el hombre no busque su deleite
> en la selva de sangre de la mañana próxima.
> El cielo tiene playas donde evitar la vida
> y hay cuerpos que no deben repetirse en la aurora.   (p. 525)

>> Because it is fair for man not to seek his delight
>> in the next morning's forest of blood.
>> Heaven has shores where life may be avoided
>> and there are bodies not to be repeated in the dawn.

Turning now to allusions to homosexual love, let us try to discover which words are more or less reliable clues to its presence. One of the indispensable clues is *oscuro* (dark). A number of friends of Lorca have referred to a collection of sonnets, now lost, called *Sonetos del amor oscuro*.[3] It is believed that many of these sonnets deal with inverted love. Once the reader is alerted to the possibility that "dark love" may convey this meaning, he finds numerous examples of *oscuro* in contexts suggesting homosexual love. If for now we limit ourselves only to *Poeta en Nueva York*, we run across the first example in "Navidad en el Hudson." Its fourth verse reads like this: "*Esa brisa de límites oscuros*" ("That breeze of dark limits"), p. 491. The next to the last verse of the same poem is a variant of the fourth: "*¡Oh brisa mía de límites que no son míos!*" ("Oh breeze of mine whose limits are not mine!"), p. 492. By remembering what was said of *brisa* in chapter 2, the reader is led to suspect

3. See Martínez Nadal's *El público*, p. 213.

that the poet speaks of love. The context of the second of these two verses confirms it. But how certain can we be that it is inverted love? The nature and frequency of other examples suggest that it is.

The most persuasive example is probably the one found in stanza 6 of "Poema doble del lago Edem," a poem in which it is impossible to doubt the presence of homosexual love. Here is the stanza:

> Pero no quiero mundo ni sueño, voz divina,
> quiero mi libertad, mi amor humano
> en el rincón más oscuro de la brisa que nadie quiera.
> ¡Mi amor humano!   (p. 499)

> But I want neither world nor dream, divine voice,
> I want my freedom, my human love
> in the darkest corner of the breeze nobody wants.
> My human love!

Each reader will have to decide for himself how persuasive a clue *oscuro* is as he continues to meet it in new combinations. In "El niño Stanton," for example, it appears as a modifier of *agua*:

> Mi agonía buscaba su traje,[4]
> polvorienta, mordida por los perros,
> y tú la acompañaste sin temblar
> hasta la puerta del agua oscura.   (p. 502)

> Dusty, bitten by dogs,
> my agony was seeking its suit,
> and you accompanied it without trembling
> as far as the gateway to dark water.

In Lorca's poetic diction, *agua* often stands for sexual desire,[5] so here is another possible example of dark love. In "Grito hacia Roma," there is a series of verses listing some places where love is found. The last one is *"en el oscurísimo beso punzante debajo de las almohadas"* ("in the darkest biting kiss beneath the pillows"), p. 521. Is this another example? The context furnishes no further clue.

But once the reader is convinced that *oscuro* may point to inverted love, he

4. See the interpretation of *traje* ventured on p. 75 of this chapter.
5. See Martínez Nadal's *El público*, p. 213.

quickly becomes aware of expressive variations. In "Paisaje de la multitud que vomita," for example, the poetic voice says:

Me defiendo con esta mirada
que mana de las ondas por donde el alba no se atreve . . .   (p. 488)

> I defend myself with this look
> that flows from the waves where dawn ventures not . . .

Clearly, the waves where dawn does not venture are "dark water." Waves, whether expressed by *ondas* or by *olas*, is another clue to be remembered. The last verse of "Paisaje de la multitud que orina" is: "*o en los cristales donde se comprenden las olas nunca repetidas*" ("or in the crystals where the never-repeated waves are understood"), p. 490. The "never-repeated waves" may well refer to fruitless love. The last verse of "Cielo vivo," which is clearly a love poem, runs: "*y amor al fin sin alba. Amor. ¡Amor visible!*" ("and love at last without dawn. Love. Visible love!"), p. 501. "Love without dawn" is surely dark love.

Another probable clue to the presence of erotic inversion is the color *azul* (blue). *Azul* is found in contexts which by themselves would lead no one to think of homosexual love. For example, in a very brief early poem from a series called "Suite de los espejos" one may read: "*¡El hombre es azul!*" ("Man is blue!"), p. 596. But one may be inclined to think back on examples of that kind once he has seen other examples in poems that treat unmistakably of dark love. Such a poem is "Oda a Walt Whitman," where these two verses occur:

Puede el hombre, si quiere, conducir su deseo
por vena de coral o celeste desnudo.   (p. 525)

> Man may, if he wishes, conduct his desire
> by vein of coral pink or (sky) blue nude.[6]

The sky blue of *celeste*, standing in contrast to coral pink, is our assurance that blue may suggest masculinity. With this in mind, one wonders at the use of *azul* in these verses from "Pequeño vals vienés":

6. Martínez Nadal thinks the references are to Aphrodite and Apollo. See *El público*, p. 177.

Hay una muerte para piano
que pinta de azul a los muchachos.   (p. 528)

> There is a death for piano
> that paints the boys blue.

By itself this *azul* is a slender basis for suspecting the presence of dark love, but there are other clues in the same poem. In its official version the poem opens with the verse *"En Viena hay diez muchachas"* ("In Vienna there are ten girls"), p. 527. But there is a published variant that substitutes "boys" for "girls."[7] And then consider the daring final verses:

Dejaré mi boca entre tus piernas,
mi alma en fotografías y azucenas,
y en las ondas oscuras de tu andar
quiero, amor mío, amor mío, dejar
violín y sepulcro, las cintas del vals.   (p. 528)

> I will leave my mouth between your legs,
> my soul in photographs and white lilies,
> and in the dark waves of your walk
> I want, my love, my love, to leave
> violin and tomb, the ribbons of the waltz.

Given this much of a basis for surmising that *azul* may express the symbolic meaning just proposed, one is inevitably led to speculate that Lorca's celebrated "blue horses" represent the drive of homosexual passion. The phrase first appears in "Tu infancia en Menton," in an obviously erotic passion already partially quoted:

Allí, león, allí furia del cielo,
te dejaré pacer en mis mejillas;
allí, caballo azul de mi locura,
pulso de nebulosa y minutero,
he de buscar las piedras de alacranes . . .   (p. 476)

> There, lion, there heaven's fury,
> I will let you graze on my cheeks;

7. See Lorca's *Obras completas*, p. 1973, for a list of variants.

there, blue horse of my madness,
pulse of nebula and minute hand,
I will seek the scorpions' stone . . .[8]

If the beloved is male, which seems likely even though it can't be proved grammatically, then blue horse does indeed evoke inverted love. In the second half of a poem called "Nocturno del hueco," in which the poetic voice seems to issue from the empty place (*hueco*) the living poet used to occupy, there is twice mentioned the *hueco* of a white horse, which may be either the white horse or the sickly pale horse of "The Revelation of John" (6.2 or 6.8). The next two verses run as follows:

No hay siglo nuevo ni luz reciente.
Solo un caballo azul y una madrugada.   (p. 509)

There is no new century or recent light.
Only a blue horse and an early dawn.

The poet's report from the far shores of death brings no new light or lasting hope but only dark love and an early dawn.

In Lorca's poetic world love, whatever its nature, is seldom a frivolous passion. On occasions it may "distribute crowns of joy," but more often it manifests itself as a deep and powerful drive and part of its power is its power to hurt. Like much of what the poet was moved to express, it is associated with dark forces emanating from some primal ground below or beyond the realm of consciousness. But this is not to say it does not show an intelligible social side as well. Some consideration of this aspect of love may help to explain its tormented character.

8. For similar rhetoric, compare these verses from one of Lorca's probable "dark sonnets":

Pero yo te sufrí. Rasgué mis venas,
tigre y paloma, sobre tu cintura
en duelo de mordiscos y azucenas.
    Llena, pues, de palabras mi locura
o déjame vivir en mi serena
noche del alma para siempre oscura.   (p. 40)

    But I put up with you. I tore my veins,
    tiger and dove, upon your waist
    in a duel of bitings and lilies.
        Fill, then, my madness with words
    or let me live in my serene
    night of the soul forever dark.

As noted in chapter 2, *Poeta en Nueva York* opens with a poem in which the poet pictures himself murdered between forms that go toward the serpent and those that seek the crystal. This is the first in a series of antitheses or polarities that contribute effectively to the mood of mystery, tension, and disquietude that characterize the book. It is often difficult to identify with certainty the opposing poles that create conflict or tension, but for the purposes of this chapter some can be identified with reasonable confidence. I have already quoted a verse that expresses the anguish felt by the poet over the conflict between his love and certain limits that are not his: "Oh breeze of mine whose limits are not mine!" (p. 491). In some cases these limits are set by norms. In the last tercet of one of Lorca's (dark?) sonnets it is suggested that his future dead body will be a *"libre signo de normas oprimidas"* ("free sign of oppressed norms"), p. 637. What are the oppressed norms? Probably those of homosexual and heterosexual love, often in conflict with each other or with the norms of society. Actually, there is a poem by Lorca titled "Normas," divided into two parts: part 1 evoking homosexual love, part 2 evoking heterosexual love (p. 648). The poet seems to express a preference for the first.[9] In the oft-quoted poem "Tu infancia en Menton," the poetic voice says to his beloved: *"Norma de amor te di, hombre de Apolo"* ("Apollo's man, I gave to thee a norm of love"), p. 475. In passing, it may be appropriate to recall that Apollo was a lover of lads (ephebes) as well as of nymphs and mortal women. But the importance of these references to *normas* is that they show that in some of his poems the poet felt love to be operating in a context of inherited standards (and taboos). By keeping this in mind, we may be able to penetrate some verses otherwise obscure.

In the New York poem called "Cielo vivo," there occur the following verses:

Allí bajo las raíces y en la médula del aire,
se comprende la verdad de las cosas equivocadas.   (p. 500)

9. See Martínez Nadal's *El público*, p. 178. He also analyzes (on pp. 183–85) another poem that deserves mention here. It is "Adán" from *Primeras canciones,* and it reveals the poet's early awareness of two kinds of love. For our purposes, it may suffice to quote the final tercet:

Pero otro Adán oscuro está soñando
neutra luna de piedra sin semilla
donde el niño de luz se irá quemando.   (p. 353)

    But another dark Adam is dreaming
    a neuter moon of stone without seed
    where the child of light will be consumed.

There neath the roots and in the marrow of the wind,
one understands the truth of mistaken things.

How typical of Lorca to try to understand the truth of what is mistaken; much of what he undertakes to express in *Poeta en Nueva York* might well be called the truth of mistaken things. A good example can be found in "Panorama ciego de Nueva York," which is an inner panorama of dark thoughts and troubled feelings about love and death. It contains some verses pertinent to our inquiry into love experienced in an atmosphere of felt social constraints. To give these verses a context, it is necessary to quote rather extensively:

Todos comprenden el dolor que se relaciona con la muerte,
pero el verdadero dolor no está en el espíritu.
No está en el aire ni en nuestra vida,
ni en estas terrazas llenas de humo.
El verdadero dolor que mantiene despiertas las cosas
es una pequeña quemadura infinita
en los ojos inocentes de otros sistemas.
   Un traje abandonado pesa tanto en los hombros
que muchas veces el cielo los agrupa en ásperas manadas.

   . . . .

Yo muchas veces me he perdido
para buscar la quemadura que mantiene despiertas las cosas
y solo he encontrado marineros echados sobre las barandillas
y pequeñas criaturas del cielo enterradas bajo la nieve.
Pero el verdadero dolor estaba en otras plazas
donde los peces cristalizados agonizaban dentro de los troncos;
plazas del cielo extraño para las antiguas estatuas ilesas
y para la tierna intimidad de los volcanes.   (p. 495)

   Everyone understands the sorrow that is related to death,
   but true sorrow is not present in the spirit.
   It is not present in the wind nor in our life,
   nor in these sidewalk cafes full of smoke.
   The true sorrow that keeps things awake
   is a small infinite burn
   in the innocent eyes of other systems.
      Cast-off suits weigh so much on the shoulders
   that heaven often gathers them in sullen herds.

      . . . .

Frequently have I lost myself
to seek the burn that keeps things awake
and I have found only sailors lolling over the railings
and heaven's little creatures buried under the snow.
But true sorrow was in other plazas
where crystalized fish were dying in the trunks;
plazas of the strange heaven for the unhurt ancient statues
and for the tender intimacy of the volcanoes.

To begin to understand what these verses are all about, we should note that the poet distinguishes two kinds of *dolor*: the easily understood sorrow related to death and another sorrow called the true one. Since in common experience there is no such thing as "true sorrow" distinguishable from all other sorrows, it is more than probable that "true" means the particular sorrow expressed in this poem. After telling us where it is not to be found, the poem first tells us, not where it is to be found, but what it is: a small infinite burn in the eyes of the other systems. "System" is the first important clue that the poem does not intend to treat of love in isolated personal terms but rather in the context of something bigger than the individuals experiencing love. What systems could these be but social systems? It is possible to speak of the innocent eyes of other systems, because innocence can be viewed as related to the accepted mores of a given system. The second important clue is the cast-off suit. If a suit stands for something prescribed or accepted by a given society, he who abandons it may find himself isolated as in the sullen herds mentioned in the poem. The last of the quoted verses are about the poet's search for the dolorous *quemadura*. Often he has gotten lost in his search, finding only sailors lolling over the railings (drunk?) and heaven's little creatures under the snow (of death). For future reference, it may be useful to note that Lorca's sailors, whether in his verse or in his drawings, are usually figures of equivocal sexuality.

Where is true sorrow to be found? The poetic voice answers in a past tense. True sorrow was in other plazas, plazas described in two ways: where crystalized fish were dying in the trunks and in the plazas of the strange heaven where ancient statues survive unhurt. The hidden meanings which I am about to venture may seem whimsical if not outrageous to some readers not steeped in Lorcan diction, but perhaps such readers will entertain as possibilities the meanings I propose until further evidence has been accumulated here and in later explications. In Lorca's poetic world, fish are occasionally phallic symbols;[10] *tronco* is now a tree trunk, now a human torso, and man is often pre-

10. See Martínez Nadal's *El público*, p. 267.

sented as though he were a tree. The sly verse containing these words evokes a phase of sexual union. The unhurt ancient statues symbolize something that has survived from the ancient world (presumably the Greek world), where the love of older men for handsome youths was an accepted part of that "other system." That this aspect of Greek culture was well known to Lorca is suggested by the first part of a poem already mentioned, namely, "Normas." Here are the pertinent verses:

Norma de ayer encontrada
sobre mi noche presente;
resplandor adolescente
que se opone a la nevada.   (p. 648)

> Yesterday's norm found
> upon my present night;
> adolescent radiance
> opposing the snowfall.

That yesterday's norm is the homosexual one suggested above is supported by its contrast with norm number two, which is that of breast and hip (*"norma de seno y cadera"*).

The key words of my analysis of fragments of "Panorama ciego de Nueva York" appear repeatedly in *Poeta en Nueva York*, not always in contexts similar to the ones that we have examined but often so. In some of them it is evident that the special suffering expressed stems from an awareness of unresolved sexual ambiguity. A good example may be taken from "Luna y panorama de los insectos," which Lorca calls a love poem:

Este fuego casto para mi deseo,
esta confusión por anhelo de equilibrio,
este inocente dolor de pólvera en mis ojos,
aliviará la angustia de otro corazón
devorado por las nebulosas.   (p. 514)

> This fire chaste compared to my yearning,
> this confusion out of longing for balance,
> this innocent sting of gunpowder in my eyes,
> will ease the anguish of another heart
> devoured by the nebulae.

Once again the poet strives to express a special kind of suffering, a suffering as sharp as gunpowder in the eyes and yet somehow innocent.[11] This suffering is accompanied by or arises out of confusion caused by a longing for balance, by a sense of being pulled in opposite directions. This is the unresolved sexual ambiguity mentioned above. Why would knowledge of such suffering relieve the anguish of another suffering heart? Because it is always a consolation not to feel alone with one's afflictions. A "heart devoured by the nebulae" is a heart consumed by something enormous yet diffuse and beyond the reach of easy understanding. Earlier in this same poem, the poet describes his own love as a "creature of devoured heart" (*"criatura de pecho devorado"*).

There is further evidence of the poet's desire to express what it is like to live a love regarded as pure yet susceptible to being confused with impure love. As is well known to students of *Poeta en Nueva York*, the poet tries in his "Oda a Walt Whitman" to establish two firmly separated categories of homosexuals. At the end of a violent attack on the ones considered corrupt, the poetic voice addresses them as follows:

Que los confundidos, los puros,
los clásicos, los señalados, los suplicantes
os cierren las puertas de la bacanal. (p. 526)

 Let the confused, the pure,
 the classic, the marked, the suppliant
 shut the bacchanal doors in your face.

Confusion is again an attribute of the homosexuals regarded as pure. The vehemence with which they are distinguished from the corrupt ones is a token of the distress that haunts their world.

We are now perhaps prepared to attempt a detailed interpretation of a key poem in the development of the theme of this chapter. Here it is in its entirety:

---

11. The combination of sorrow and pain and something akin to innocence is typical of these poems. Here is an example from "Oda a Walt Whitman":

soñabas ser un río y dormir como un río
con aquel camarada que pondría en tu pecho
un pequeño dolor de ignorante leopardo. (p. 524)

 you dreamed of being a river and sleeping like a river
 with that comrade who would put in your heart
 a liitle pain of ignorant leopard.

In this case "ignorant" is roughly equivalent to "innocent."

Poema Doble del Lago Edem

1   *Era mi voz antigua*
     ignorante de los densos jugos amargos.
     La adivino lamiendo mis pies
     bajo los frágiles helechos mojados.

2   *¡Ay voz antigua de mi amor,*
     ay voz de mi verdad,
     ay voz de mi abierto costado,
     cuando todas las rosas manaban de mi lengua
     y el césped no conocía la impasible dentadura del caballo!

3   *Estás aquí bebiendo mi sangre,*
     bebiendo mi humor de niño pesado,
     mientras mis ojos se quiebran en el viento
     con el aluminio y las voces de los borrachos.

4   *Déjame pasar la puerta*
     donde Eva come hormigas
     y Adán fecunda peces deslumbrados.
     Déjame pasar hombrecillos de los cuernos
     al bosque de los desperezos
     y los alegrísimos saltos.

5   *Yo sé el uso más secreto*
     que tiene un viejo alfiler oxidado
     y sé del horror de unos ojos despiertos
     sobre la superficie concreta del plato.

6   *Pero no quiero mundo ni sueño, voz divina,*
     quiero mi libertad, mi amor humano
     en el rincón más oscuro de la brisa que nadie quiera.
     ¡Mi amor humano!

7   *Esos perros marinos se persiguen*
     y el viento acecha troncos descuidados.
     ¡Oh voz antigua, quema con tu lengua
     esta voz de hojalata y de talco!

8   *Quiero llorar porque me da la gana*
     como lloran los niños del último banco,
     porque yo no soy un hombre, ni un poeta, ni una hoja,
     pero sí un pulso herido que sonda las cosas del otro lado.

9   *Quiero llorar diciendo mi nombre,*
    rosa, niño y abeto a la orilla de este lago,
    para decir mi verdad de hombre de sangre
    matando en mí la burla y sugestión del vocablo.

10   *No, no, yo no pregunto, yo deseo,*
    voz mía libertada que me lames las manos.
    En el laberinto de biombos es mi desnudo el que recibe
    la luna de castigo y el reloj encenizado.

11   *Así hablaba yo.*
    Así hablaba yo cuando Saturno detuvo los trenes
    y la bruma y el Sueño y la Muerte me estaban buscando.
    Me estaban buscando
    allí donde mugen las vacas que tienen patitas de paje
    y allí donde flota mi cuerpo entre los equilibrios contrarios.   (pp. 498–99)

Double Poem of Lake Eden

1   It was my former voice
    ignorant of the thick bitter juices.
    I divine it licking my feet
    under the fragile damp ferns.

2   Oh former voice of my love,
    oh voice of my truth,
    oh voice of my wounded side,
    when all the roses flowed from my tongue
    and the turf knew not the impassive teeth of the horse!

3   Here you are drinking my blood,
    drinking my tiresome child's humor,
    while my eyes break in the wind
    with the aluminum and the drunkards' words.

4   Let me pass through the gate
    where Eve eats ants
    and Adam impregnates dazzled fish.
    Let me pass little horned men
    to the grove of the stretches
    and the merriest leaps.

5   I know the most secret use
    that an old rusty pin has

and I know the horror of wide-awake eyes
over the concrete surface of the plate.

6   But I want neither world nor dream, divine voice,
I want my freedom, my human love
in the darkest corner of the breeze nobody wants,
My human love!

7   Those sea dogs pursue one another
and the wind stalks careless trunks.
Oh ancient voice, burn with your tongue
this voice of tin and tinsel!

8   I want to cry because I feel like it
as the children on the back bench cry,
because I am neither man, nor poet, nor leaf,
but a wounded pulse probing things from the other side.

9   I want to cry saying my name,
rose, child and fir on the shore of this lake,
to say my truth of a man of blood
killing in myself the mockery and suggestion of the word.

10   No, no, I do not question, I desire,
liberated voice of mine that licks my hands,
In the labyrinth of screens it is my nude that receives
the punishing moon and the clock covered with ashes.

11   Thus was I speaking.
Thus was I speaking when Saturn stopped the trains
and mist and Dream and Death were looking for me.
They were looking for me
where cows with pages' tiny feet were mooing
and where my body floats between balanced opposites.

This poem was written in late August of 1929, after the poet had already spent some time in New York City. The title tells us two things: that the poetic setting is the shore of a lake in Vermont called "Lake Eden,"[12] and

12. Since part of what the poem expresses is nostalgia for a time of innocence, it may seem appropriate that "Eden" should figure in the title of the poem; but, as we shall see, the poet asks to go, not back to the Garden of Eden, but to the place where Adam and Eve now ignore each other. It is probable that "Eden" became part of the title of the poem, mostly because the lake visited by the poet really does bear the name of Lake Eden. For about ten days in August 1929 Lorca visited the young American poet and friend, Philip Cummings, at Eden Mills, Vermont. Readers interested in learning more about Lorca's

that the poem is in some sense double. The most obvious doubleness is the double temporal perspective with which the poem opens. Less obvious are the double meanings that emerge from a careful reading.

Under the title of the poem, Lorca quoted a verse from Garcilaso's Second Eclogue: "*Nuestro ganado pace, el viento espira*" ("Our cattle graze, the wind dies down"). This tranquil verse and the pastoral setting of rural Vermont seem to augur some respite from the turmoil of the city if not from the personal preoccupations that still torment the poet's spirit. In this natural setting the poet senses the presence of his former voice, a voice which in stanza 1 he characterizes as ignorant of the thick bitter juices that afflict his present self. Why does it manifest itself as a being that licks the poet's feet under the fragile ferns? Perhaps the intended image is that of a faithful and fawning dog come to comfort his troubled master. The ferns, being shy forest plants, evoke the seclusion appropriate to intimate communion.

In stanza 2 the poet, still addressing his former voice, calls it a voice of love, of truth, but also of noble suffering. Since the "wounded side" is figurative, it is surely a reference to the crucified Christ, the highest representation of suffering for love. The temporal perspective of the former voice is that of a time when his tongue flowed with roses and the horse of erotic passion did not yet know the grass of death.[13] The tongue flowing with roses is clearly a positive symbol. Lorca used it in another New York poem ("Ciudad sin sueño") in a context of hopeful prophecy. But since the poet is addressing his former voice, perhaps it is legitimate to think back to a youthful poem (dated 7 May 1918) called "La oración de las rosas" (pp. 579–82). In this early poem roses are already characteristically ambiguous, They are: "*polen de la luna*" ("moon pollen"), "*flor de Dios y Luzbel*" ("flower of God and Lucifer"), "*las mujeres entre todas las flores*" ("the women among all the flowers"), "*la poesía que es un agua de vuestros rosales*" ("poetry which is a water of your rosebushes"), and, most insistently, "*flores de amor*" ("flowers of love"). It is hard to say how many of the values here listed are intended in the stanza under consideration, but at least two seem certain: poetry and love.

In stanza 3 the poet continues to address his former voice, which is of course a way of referring to his earlier self. What does he mean by saying that his former voice is drinking his blood and his childish ill humor? Although the

---

sojourn in Vermont may consult the recently published *Songs by García Lorca*, translated by Cummings and edited by Daniel Eisenberg (Pittsburgh: Duquesne University Press, 1976). Also: Kessel Schwartz, "García Lorca en Vermont," *Hispania* 42 (1959): 50–55.

13. Martínez Nadal has studied *hierba* as agent and symbol of death. See his *El público*, pp. 118–22.

phrase *beber sangre a uno* usually expresses hatred and a desire for revenge, that does not appear to be a possible meaning here. Perhaps it means that his former self is absorbing or learning about his present passionate unhappiness while his present self is blinded and confused by elements standing for his New York experience: the aluminum and the drunkards' words.

In stanza 4 the poet asks to escape into another world described in two ways: a world where Adam and Eve ignore each other and a world where little men with horns leap merrily about the forest. It is not certain what the activities of Adam and Eve are meant to suggest. In Lorcan symbolism, *hormigas* are usually negative elements, sometimes associated with sterility and death;[14] *peces* are occasionally sexual symbols. What seems clear is that the poet does not ask to return to the Garden of Eden but to the place where the exiled first man and woman no longer show any interest in each other. The second world is surely the Arcadian groves where Pan and the lascivious satyrs made merry. One is tempted to believe that the forest is the *selva sagrada* of unbridled sensuality celebrated in Rubén Darío's "Yo soy aquel . . ."

Stanza 5 is particularly obscure. The first two verses seem to point to something arcane; the second, to something commonplace. On a guess, one might say that the secret use of a rusty old pin belongs to the lore of sympathetic magic, that of the gypsies or the blacks. The horror of wide-awake eyes over the surface of a plate may be the horror of routine domesticity. Whatever it is that the poet claims to know in this stanza is virtually annulled in the following stanza. Still speaking to his former voice, now called divine, he exclaims: "But I want neither world nor dream. . . ." What he does want is freedom to love in his own human way in the darkest corner of the breeze. The dark breeze is inverted love. The repeated stress on the word "human" raises this dark love above that of the corrupt fairies of the big city so fiercely castigated in the "Oda a Walt Whitman."[15]

14. Moraima Semprun Donahue claims, without adducing evidence, that *hormigas* commonly represent women in Lorca's writings, which might possibly be so in this instance but ordinarily is not so. For an extravagantly Freudian interpretation of some of the New York poems, see her "Cristo en Lorca," *Explicación de textos literarios* 4 (1975–76): 23–24.

15. Long after I wrote this chapter, I came across a revealing newspaper article by Cipriano Rivas Cherif, who was a theater director and friend of Lorca's in the 1930s. In the article Rivas Cherif records a confidential conversation with Lorca in which Lorca revealed to him his true sexual nature. I quote a portion of the conversation because of its close relevance to some of the matters discussed in this chapter. Here are Lorca's pertinent words as remembered and published by Rivas Cherif:

The fact of the matter, if what you say is true, is that you are as abnormal as I am. Because in fact I am. Because I have known only men; and you know that the homo-

The key words of the first two verses of stanza 7 are *perros marinos*. In standard Spanish these are dogfish, a variety of small shark. They could readily be conceived as pursuing one another, but this idea contributes nothing to the meaning of the poem and it can't be related to verse 2. To test a more appropriate meaning, let us suppose that "sea dogs" are sailors. Lorca could have learned in New York this meaning of the English phrase "sea dogs." If he did, it would help to explain the obscure *perros* found in three other New York poems. From "El niño Stanton," we have already quoted the phrase *"mordida por los perros"* ("bitten by dogs"). In "Nocturno del hueco" one finds this enigmatic verse: *"Perros equivocados y manzanas mordidas"* ("Mistaken dogs and bitten apples"), p. 508. Remembering the symbolic value of *manzana* discussed in chapter 2, we realize that these mistaken (sea) dogs are associated in this laconic verse with consummated sex.[16] The other mysterious *perros* are those of verse 5 in "Crucifixión": *"Cojos perros fumaban sus pipas . . ."* ("Lame dogs were smoking their pipes . . ."). Is it not plausible to assume that these dogs are old sea dogs smoking their pipes? Returning to stanza 7, if the *perros marinos* are sailors pursuing one another, verse 2 echoes and makes more explicit this meaning: the wind of erotic passion stalks careless torsos. Verses 3 and 4 appeal to his former voice to burn with its tongue (fulminate against) the vulgar world of promiscuous sexuality with which his present voice is confronted.

In stanza 3 the poet speaks of his humor as that of a tiresome child. Now in stanza 8 his urge to cry is compared to that of school children relegated to

---

sexual, the fairy makes me laugh, amuses me with his womanish itch to wash, iron and sew, to paint himself, to wear skirts, to speak with effeminate faces and gestures. But I don't like it. Normality is neither your way of knowing only women, or mine. What's normal is love without limits. Because love is more and better than the morality of a dogma, Catholic morality; there is no one can make me resign myself to the sole stance of having children. In my way there is no misrepresentation. Both are as they are. Without switching. There is no one who gives orders; there is no one who dominates; there is no submission. There is no assigning of roles. There is no substitution or imitation. There is only abandon and joyous mutual possession. But it would take a real revolution. A new morality, a morality of complete freedom. That is what Walt Whitman was asking for. And that may be the freedom the New World will proclaim: the heterosexualism in which America lives. Just like the ancient world.

Trans. from "La muerte y la pasión de Federico García Lorca," *Excelsior* (Mexico), 13 Jan. 1957, on p. 4 of the section called "Diorama de la cultura."

16. If the reader wonders in what sense these "sea dogs" are mistaken, it may help to recall two verses from "pequeño poema infinito": *"Equivocar el camino/ es llegar a la mujer"* ("To mistake the way is to come to woman"), p. 531.

the back bench, that is to say, children isolated from their fellows, which hints again at the social aspect of inverted love. But the poet wants to cry also because he doesn't know exactly who or what he is: nor man, nor poet, nor leaf. Here it may be appropriate to recall that *Poeta en Nueva York* opens with a poem expressing a similar uncertainty: *"Tropezando con mi rostro distinto de cada día"* ("Stumbling upon my different face each day"). What the poet does identify in the powerful final verse of stanza 8 is his most elementary and suffering biological self probing some ulterior world.

Still under the impulse to weep, in stanza 9 the poet is moved to unburden himself of a personal truth that is part of his torment. When he says that on the shore of Lake Eden his name is "rose, child and fir," he identifies himself with the simple natural world, but the last two verses reveal that the social aspect of "the bitter juices" is still at work. He wants to speak his personal truth as a man of passion. What that truth is here conceived to be is expressed in the final verse of the stanza: "Killing in myself the mockery and suggestion of the word." The troubling word is not hard to imagine in the context just reviewed.

In stanza 10 the poet calls the caressing voice of earlier times his "liberated voice," liberated because now able to express more freely in his poetry what previously was alluded to more obscurely. In the first verse he proclaims the predominance (for him) of desire over inquiry. The right to desire is his, since it will be his true self (*mi desnudo*) that suffers the punishing moon and the clock covered with ashes. A crucial phrase not yet commented on is *"en el laberinto de biombos."* *Biombo* (screen) is used only in this one poem of *Poeta en Nueva York*. However, it is a key word in Lorca's recently published play, *El público*. The editor, R. Martínez Nadal, has called attention to the magic screen used by some of the characters in the play to unmask the homosexual character of others.[17] The fourth verse of stanza 10 implies that the poet's true nature will be disclosed in a labyrinth of such screens.

In the final stanza the poet imagines his inner colloquy with himself coming to an end as a god of the ancient world stopped the machines of the modern world, and mist, dream, and death were looking for him in an undefined place of sexual ambiguity, a place where his body floats between balanced opposites. More than once in *Poeta en Nueva York* the lowing of a cow is the cry of a victim. In this particular poem the cow is appropriately hermaphroditic, having

17. Martínez Nadal discusses *biombo* in *El público*, p. 43; but the reader can now judge for himself how it is used. See the same author's recent edition of García Lorca: *Autógrafos II, El público* (Oxford: The Dolphin Book Co., 1976), pp. xvii-xix.

the tiny feet of a pageboy. It is probably no accident that the first and last stanzas contain the notion of feet. It was feet that the caressing voice of the poet's earlier self came to console. The second reference to feet completes and confirms the doubleness hidden in "Poema doble del lago Edem."

The most explicit treatment of the theme of dark love is found in the "Oda a Walt Whitman." I have already found occasion to quote from it several times. To attempt now a full analysis of it would involve much repetition. But there is a stanza that may contribute something more to our understanding of the theme of tormented love. It occurs between stanzas 13 and 15, which are the ones most often quoted by critics, probably because they contain the undisguised expression of the double outlet for human eroticism. Stanza 14 runs as follows:

> Agonía, agonía, sueño, fermento y sueño.
> Este es el mundo, amigo, agonía, agonía.
> Los muertos se descomponen bajo el reloj de las ciudades,
> la guerra pasa llorando con un millón de ratas grises,
> los ricos dan a sus queridas
> pequeños moribundos iluminados,
> y la vida no es noble, ni buena, ni sagrada.   (p. 525)

> Agony, agony, dream, ferment and dream.
> This is the world, friend, agony, agony.
> The dead rot under the clock of the cities,
> war passes weeping with a million gray rats,
> the rich give to their mistresses
> little ones dying and enlightened,
> and life is not noble, or good, or sacred.

The treatment of the theme of inverted love is brusquely interrupted by this bleak characterization of the world as mostly agony, where life is neither noble, nor good, nor sacred. Three negative elements are mentioned: death, war, and futile procreation. On the surface these would appear to have no necessary connection with the theme of dark love, but everywhere in *Poeta en Nueva York* such combinations are present. The bitter emotions expressed by the poet are entangled in the intimate interplay of his personal problem with all that he found ignoble and distressing in the city. But of course death is the sovereign aggravator of the torment of love, especially death felt to be irredeemable. We will conclude this chapter with a look at a poem that illustrates this point. It is called "Ruina" and fits appropriately into the section called "Introducción a la muerte":

1   *Sin encontrarse.*
     Viajero por su propio torso blanco.
     Así iba el aire.

2   *Pronto se vio que la luna*
     era una calavera de caballo
     y el aire una manzana oscura.

3   *Detrás de la ventana*
     con látigos y luces, se sentía
     la lucha de la arena con el agua.

4   *Yo vi llegar las hierbas*
     y les eché un cordero que balaba
     bajo sus dientecillos y lancetas.

5   *Volaba dentro de una gota*
     la cáscara de pluma y celuloide
     de la primer paloma.

6   *Las nubes, en manada,*
     se quedaron dormidas contemplando
     el duelo de las rocas con el alba.

7   *Vienen las hierbas, hijo;*
     ya suenan sus espadas de saliva
     por el cielo vacío.

8   *Mi mano, amor. ¡Las hierbas!*
     Por los cristales rotos de la casa
     la sangre desató sus cabelleras.

9   *Tú solo y yo quedamos;*
     prepara tu esqueleto para el aire.
     Yo solo y tú quedamos.

10   *Prepara tu esqueleto;*
     hay que buscar de prisa, amor, de prisa,
     nuestro perfil sin sueño.

(pp. 510–11)

1   Without finding itself.
     Traveler along its own white torso.
     So went the wind.

2   Soon it was seen that the moon
     was a horse's skull
     and the wind a dark apple.

3   Behind the window,
     with lashes and lights, was sensed
     the fight of the sand with the water.

4   I saw the grasses arrive
     and I tossed them a lamb bleating
     under their little teeth and lancets.

5   Flying in a drop of water
     was the shell of feather and celluloid
     of the first dove.

6   The clouds in a flock
     fell asleep contemplating
     the duel of the rocks with the dawn.

7   The grasses are coming, son;
     the swords of their spittle are already sounding
     through the empty sky.

8   My hand, love. The grasses!
     Through the broken windows of the house
     blood let down its tresses.

9   You alone and I remain;
     prepare your skeleton for the wind.
     I alone and you remain.

10   Prepare your skeleton;
     Swiftly must we seek, love, swiftly
     our dreamless profile.

Stanzas 1 and 2 serve to characterize the wind, which is of course the amorous breeze so often referred to in these pages. It is a random energy attentive only to itself. It used to be the dark apple of inverted love, but it was soon seen that the horse of erotic passion was to be a skull equated with the moon of death.

The poet and his lover are briefly sheltered by a window from the inescapable ruin of everything. On the other side of the window they sense with pain (*látigos*) and understanding (*luces*) the struggle of sand and water, which is the struggle of death and sterility with sexual desire.

In stanza 4 the poet says he saw the grasses arrive and he tossed them a lamb. As previously noted, the grasses are usually heralds or agents of death. What lamb would he throw to the agents of death and with what purpose? The lamb suffering under the teeth of death is surely an allusion to the cruci-fied Christ, who is the supreme example of dying for love.

Another Christian allusion is present in stanza 5. It is what little can be detected of the shell of the first dove, which, coming on the heels of the allu-sion to the lamb of God, is plausibly an evocation of the Holy Ghost. In the form of its appearance in this poem, it does not seem to offer much hope or consolation.

In stanza 6 the indifferent clouds fall asleep watching the duel of death (*rocas*) and rebirth (*alba*). And then in stanza 7 the poet announces to his beloved the advent of the menacing grasses through the empty sky. Does the sky seem empty because Christ's sacrifice was in vain and so little can be seen of the spirit of God?

In stanza 8 the poet offers his hand to his love as he cries out "the grasses!" This seems to express in brief a feeling more fully developed in a later poem called "Casida de la mano imposible," of which I quote two verses:

Yo no quiero más que esa mano
para tener un ala de mi muerte.   (p. 572)

> I want only that hand
> to hold a wing of my death.

But the loving hand affords no stay against inpending ruin. The windows of the house, which at first separated the lovers from the struggle of life and death, are now broken and the blood of life and passion begins to ebb.

In the last two stanzas the poet speaks of his lover's skeleton, which is an expressive way of drawing the fatal future into the urgent present. The shelter-ing windows being broken, only the lovers remain. What does it mean for the poet to tell his love to prepare his skeleton for the wind? To prepare for love despite the certainty of death? The second time he tells him to prepare his skeleton, he adds that they must swiftly seek their dreamless profile, that is, their true identity as lovers doomed to irredeemable death.

6

Abandoned church

From beginning to end Lorca's writings reflect an extensive religious culture, including frequent references to God and the Devil, to Christ, to the Catholic Church and its liturgy, to Biblical personages and stories, to the Saints and Martyrs. In most of his published interviews and letters allusions to God are mostly conventional and they afford no persuasive hint of loss of faith. His poetry is different. In his very first published collection there are many poems that raise questions about God's accessibility to man and about the poet's personal doubts. As early as 1918, in a poem called "Los encuentros de un caracol aventurero," the reader learns that two old frogs, who insist the snail believe in eternal life, do not believe in it themselves (p. 178). Although this poem does not necessarily implicate the poet's own religious attitudes, he was soon writing poems that do. In a youthful poem titled "Prólogo" the poet threatens to make a pact with Satan if God continues to ignore him (pp. 240–43). In "Manantial" he asserts that God's beacon has gone out (p. 273). In "Ritmo de otoño" loss of faith is explicit:

En mi alma perdiéronse solemnes
carne y alma de Cristo   (p. 284)

> In my soul were solemnly lost
> flesh and soul of Christ.

And on the same page:

Y tengo la amargura solitaria
de no saber mi fin ni mi destino.

> And I have the solitary bitterness
> of not knowing my end or my destiny.

These few examples have not been adduced to imply that at the time Lorca was composing his first poems he had permanently lost his religious faith. There are other early poems that treat religious motifs with no sign of flagging faith. It is apparent, though, that in his earliest writings he was already plagued by the uncertainty of God's Grace. By the time he was writing *Poeta en Nueva York*, it was an abiding preoccupation.

Most of the major themes treated by Lorca in his New York poems show a social or institutional side as well as an intimately personal one. The personal side of the religious theme looms larger than the other side in *Poeta en Nueva York*, but the other is present and should be examined. Although its sometimes veiled presence can be detected in a number of poems, it appears most prominently in two: "Cementerio judío" and "Grito hacia Roma." The first of these poems is mostly about the fate of the persecuted Jews, but, significantly, the children of Christ are brought into the poem five times: three times they are presented as sleeping, once as singing and once as rowing. Since the poem is about the persecution and suffering of the Jews, the above-mentioned references to the children of Christ must mean that the Christians either participated in the persecution or were indifferent to it. In other words, the poem is to some degree an indictment of Christianity.

"Grito hacia Roma" is a bitter cry hurled at the capital of Christendom from the tower of the Chrysler Building in New York. In the first stanza a portion of what the poet finds to be evil or distressing in the modern urban world is presented as a kind of retribution that will descend on Rome. At the end of the stanza there is a veiled reference to a widely reported historical event that occurred a few months before the poet's arrival in New York. I quote the pertinent verses:

Caerán sobre la gran cúpula
que untan de aceite las lenguas militares
donde un hombre se orina en una deslumbrante paloma
y escupe carbón machacado
rodeado de miles de campanillas.   (p. 520)

> They will fall on the great cupola
> that military tongues anoint with oil
> where a man passes water on a dazzling dove
> and spits out pulverized coal
> surrounded by thousands of little bells.

The great cupola is surely that of St. Peter's Church in Rome and the man who defiles the dazzling dove (the Holy Spirit) is Mussolini. The historical reference can only be to the Lateran Treaty signed by Mussolini and a papal representative.[1] It is evident that the poet did not approve of this pact between the Holy See and the Fascist government of Italy. In the second half of the poem the Pope is clearly present:

Pero el viejo de las manos traslúcidas
dirá: amor, amor, amor,
aclamado por millones de moribundos;
dirá: amor, amor, amor,
entre el tisú estremecido de ternura;
dirá: paza, paz, paz,
entre el tirite de cuchillos y melones de dinamita;
dirá: amor, amor, amor,
hasta que se le pongan de plata los labios.   (p. 521)

> But the old man of the translucent hands
> will say: love, love, love,
> acclaimed by the dying millions;
> he will say: love, love, love,
> in his silk vestment atremble with tenderness;
> he will say: peace, peace, peace,
> in the shiver of knives and dynamite melons;
> he will say: love, love, love,
> until his lips are covered with silver.

1. At least two scholars have noticed this fact: Fusero, p. 294; and Laffranque, p. 227, n. 87.

The highest earthly representative of the Roman Church proclaims love and peace in a world of violence and death. Institutionalized religion, then, is viewed as ineffectual in such a world.

Since God's role in human lives is an important theme in the New York poems, it is singularly appropriate that the collection should open with a poem that assigns to God the responsibility for the poet's imagined death. It will be instructive to return to this heaven-willed death to inquire what its deepest meaning may be, but, for now, let us simply recall how insistently the poet refers to his own death. The notion of his murder is repeated in "Fábula y rueda de los tres amigos" (p. 475); in "Danza de la muerte" the poet pictures himself on a terrace struggling with the moon of death (p. 486); in "Navidad en el Hudson" the person with his throat cut turns out to be the poet himself (p. 492); in "Poema doble del lago Edem," he imagines himself on the shore of Lake Eden where mist and Dream and Death were seeking him out (p. 499); in "Nocturno del hueco" he speaks of and from the empty place (hueco) he once occupied in the air (p. 508). Obviously, a death so repeatedly anticipated bulks large in the poetic experience of New York. Is there some sense in which it can be conceived as God's responsibility? To find at least a part of the answer, we must turn to "Iglesia abandonada":

Iglesia Abandonada
(Balada de la Gran Guerra)

1 Yo tenía un hijo que se llamaba Juan.
   Yo tenía un hijo.
3 Se perdió por los arcos un viernes de todos los muertos.
   Le vi jugar en las últimas escaleras de la misa
5 y echaba un cubito de hojalata en el corazón del sacerdote.
   He golpeado los ataúdes. ¡Mi hijo! ¡Mi hijo! ¡Mi hijo!
7 Saqué una pata de gallina por detrás de la luna y luego,
   comprendí que mi niña era un pez
9 por donde se alejan las carretas.
   Yo tenía una niña.
11 Yo tenía un pez muerto bajo las cenizas de los incensarios.
   Yo tenía un mar. ¿De qué? ¡Dios mío! ¡Un mar!
13 Subí a tocar las campanas, pero las frutas tenían gusanos
   y las cerillas apagadas
15 se comían los trigos de primavera.
   Yo vi la transparente cigüeña de alcohol

17 *mondar las negras cabezas de los soldados agonizantes*
y vi las cabañas de goma
19 *donde giraban las copas llenas de lágrimas.*
En las anémonas del ofertorio te encontraré, ¡corazón mío!,
21 *cuando el sacerdote levante la mula y el buey con sus fuertes brazos*
para espantar los sapos nocturnos que rondan los helados paisajes del cáliz.
23 *Yo tenía un hijo que era un gigante,*
pero los muertos son más fuertes y saben devorar pedazos del cielo.
25 *Si mi niño hubiera sido un oso,*
yo no temería el sigilo de los caimanes,
27 *ni hubiese visto el mar amarrado a los árboles*
para ser fornicado y herido por el tropel de los regimientos.
29 *¡Si mi niño hubiera sido un oso!*
Me envolveré sobre esta lona dura para no sentir el frío de los musgos.
31 *Sé muy bien que me darán una manga o la corbata;*
pero en el centro de la misa yo romperé el timón y entonces
vendrá a la piedra la locura de pingüinos y gaviotas
33 *que harán decir a los que duermen y a los que cantan por las esquinas:*
él tenía un hijo.
35 *¡Un hijo! ¡Un hijo! ¡Un hijo!*
que no era más que suyo, porque era su hijo!
37 *¡Su hijo! ¡Su hijo! ¡Su hijo!*   (pp. 482–83)

Abandoned Church
(Ballad of the Great War)

1 I had a son named John.
I had a son.
3 He was lost through the arches on a Friday of all the dead.
I saw him playing on the last stairs of the mass
5 and he was tossing a little tin pail on the heart of the priest
I have pounded on the coffins. My son! my son! my son!
7 I pulled a chicken's leg from behind the moon and then,
I understood that my little girl was a fish
9 along where the carts draw away.
I had a little girl.
11 I had a fish dead under the ashes of the censers.
I had a sea. Of what? My God! A sea!

13 I climbed up to ring the bells, but the fruits were wormy
and the extinguished tapers
15 were consuming the spring wheat.
I saw the transparent stork of alcohol
17 trimming the black heads of the dying soldiers
and I saw the huts of rubber
19 where the cups full of tears went round.
In the anemones of the offertory I shall find you, my heart!,
21 when the priest lifts the mule and the ox with his strong arms
to scare away the nocturnal toads that prowl about the icy landscapes of
the chalice.
23 I had a son who was a giant,
but the dead are stronger and they can devour pieces of heaven.
25 If my little boy had been a bear,
I would not fear the stealth of the alligators,
27 nor would I have seen the sea lashed to the trees
to be ravished and wounded by the throng of the regiments.
29 If my son had been a bear!
I'll wrap myself up on this hard canvas not to feel the cold of the mosses.
31 I know very well that they will give me a sleeve or the necktie;
but in the center of the mass I will break the rudder and then
33 there will come to the stone the madness of penguins and gulls
that will make those who sleep and those who sing on the corners say:
35 he had a son,
A son! A son! A son!
37 who was his alone, because it was his son!
His son! His son! His son!

"Iglesia abandonada" is a difficult poem for a number of special reasons. Since it has nothing to do with blacks, one may wonder whether its inclusion in the section called "Los Negros" is an accident of the posthumous publication of *Poeta en Nueva York* or whether it is a ruse to hide the deeper meaning of the poem from all but the most discerning readers. Does the subtitle, "Ballad of the Great War," contribute to the reader's understanding of the poem or is it a deliberate distraction? In the body of the poem, the poet manipulates a good deal of reasonably clear religious material, but he also introduces seemingly incongruous elements. Do these elements clarify the religious import of the poem or were they intended to obscure it? When enough painstaking work has been done on Lorcan symbolism and when it becomes possible (if it ever does) to see the original manuscript, some of these questions may receive definitive answers. In the meantime it seems possible to offer a plausible interpretation of the overall significance of the poem.

The poet begins by asserting that he used to have a son named John, who was lost through the arches on a Friday of all the dead. Even if we did not know enough of Lorca's life to be confident he never had a son of flesh and blood, we would soon realize that the son here referred to is a wholly figurative one. Let us assume provisionally that he is, in a sense later to be defined, the boy the poet used to be. Let us further assume that he called him John in remembrance of John the Baptist, who may stand for firm faith in Jesus Christ. In Lorcan symbolism, to pass through the arches is ordinarily to die.[2] And so the third verse means that his son died on a Friday of all the dead. Friday was the day of Christ's crucifixion. If His sacrifice for our redemption failed of its purpose, then Friday would indeed be the day of all the dead, the irredeemable dead. Verses 4 and 5 are the first to introduce seemingly incongruous elements into the poem. The word *escaleras* may be a substitute for *gradas* (altar steps) where the antiphon called the gradual is sung, but since it is not the normal word for "altar steps," it is probably intended to suggest other meanings. *Escaleras* may be ladders. If that is the meaning here intended, does it allude to Jacob's Heaven-reaching ladder or to the ladders associated in Christian art with the descent from the Cross? Quite possibly verses 4 and 5 allude to Lorca's childhood practice of playing priest and saying mass.[3] I remember no account of the altar ornaments and sacred vessels used by the child Lorca when he played at saying mass. Is it possible that the little tin pail mentioned in verse 5 represents the chalice he then used? Real chalices are, of course, made of precious metals to be worthy to hold the precious blood of Christ. To recall the tin pail in the context of this despairing poem may be to downgrade a chalice no longer held to serve a believable function. In any case the little tin pail tossed (poured?) on the heart of the priest can hardly be anything but negative. In verse 6 the poet searches for his son, but pounding on the coffins brings no response from the dead.

For now verse 7 remains obscure. To pull a chicken leg from behind the moon sounds like the hocus-pocus of primitive incantation. It is followed by a series of images standing for different aspects of whatever "son" is intended to represent. The girl-child (*niña*) mentioned in verse 8 may recall to some readers the *alma niña* of one of Antonio Machado's early poems; in any event,

2. Martínez Nadal, in *El público . . .*, pp. 117–22, has noted the association of *arcos* with death.

3. See Marcelle Auclair, *Enfances et mort de García Lorca* (Paris: Editions du Seuill, 1968), p. 52.

may it not evoke the candor and fragility of childhood faith?[4] But then the poet understood that the child was a fish along the place where the carts draw away. Given the religious context, the fish is probably a symbol of baptism, as it sometimes is in early Christian literature and art; but it is a baptism from which people now draw away. After repeating that he had a girl-child, the poet says he had a dead fish under the ashes of the censers, which is to say, baptism that failed of its purpose under the ashes of extinguished prayers. The image then changes to sea. Sea of what?, he asks but does not answer. A plausible answer would be the vast emptiness of death.

In line 13 the poet climbed up to ring the bells, but the fruits were wormy and the extinguished tapers were consuming the spring wheat. Perhaps these verses should be considered in the light of certain words from the preaching of John the Baptist: "Already the axe is laid to the roots of the trees; and every tree that fails to produce good fruit is cut and thrown on the fire. . . . His [Jesus'] shovel is ready in his hand and he will winnow his threshing floor; the wheat he will gather into his granary, but he will burn the chaff on a fire that can never go out" (Math. 3.10–12). The chief difference between what John prophesies and what the poet reports is that the former foretells the burning of the chaff (the unrepentant sinners), whereas the latter states that the young wheat itself was consumed by fire, that is, even the good cannot escape extinction. But there may be another way to interpret these verses. The little bells may be Sanctus bells rung at the altar to announce the coming of Christ in the Eucharist. The *cerillas* may be the Eucharistic candles that symbolize the coming of Christ in the communion. But the fruits are wormy (unworthy)

---

4. A. Machado uses the phrase "el alma niña" in a poem titled "Renacimiento" from *Soledades, galerías y otros poemas*. One may think of another mysterious *niña*, who appears in Lorca's "Crucifixión." These verses appear toward the end of that poem:

Porque la luna lavó con agua
las quemaduras de los caballos
y no la niña viva que callaron en la arena.   (p. 533)

    Because the moon washed with water
    the horses' burns
    and not the living girl silenced in the sand.

If this *niña* also stands for childhood faith, the reconciliation of love and death expressed in these verses does not include the hope traditionally associated with the Crucifixion. C. Marcilly interprets this *niña* as that part of Christ representing "tenderness, love and harmony in love." See his "Notes pour l'Étude de la Pensée Religieuse de F. García Lorca: Crucifixión," in *Bulletin Hispanique*, 64 bis (1962): 521–22.

and the candles are out and the wheat (flour) Host) Christ) is being destroyed.[5] Whatever the correct interpretation of these verses may be, who can doubt that they are strongly negative?

The images found in verses 16–19 seem intended to convey the absurd horror of World War I. Possibly no symbolism is intended in them; but, if some is intended, it may be that the Annunciation (the stork) is only an alcoholic emanation whereas death and sorrow are real.

Only past tenses occur in the verses studied up to this point, but suddenly the poet switches to the future:

> In the anemones of the offertory I shall find you, my heart!,
> when the priest lifts the mule and the ox with his strong arms
> to scare away the nocturnal toads that prowl about the icy landscapes of the chalice.

At first glance the reader may catch a glimmer of hope in these lines, but careful examination shows none. In pagan times the anemone was already a symbol of sorrow and death (derived from the death of Adonis); in Christian symbolism the red spots on the petals are the blood of Christ. And so the poet foretells the finding of his heart (his lost son) in the blood of Christ (as represented in the offertory) when the priest lifts (expressed by the present subjunctive in the sense of indefinite future) the mule and the ox. In this part of the mass, it is of course the sacramental bread and wine that are raised by the priest, not the mule and the ox. The unexpected inclusion of these animals obliges the reader to pause and ponder their possible meaning. If the poet meant to evoke in the priest's reenactment of Christ's sacrifice both the Crucifixion and the Nativity (a union so often found in Lorca's poetic world), the traditional pair of animals to suggest the Nativity would be the ass and the ox.[6] By substituting mule for ass, the poet directs attention to what mule and ox have in common, namely, sterility. And so it appears that Christ's sacrifice was sterile and will not be effective in frightening evil spirits away from the icy (another form of sterility) landscapes of the chalice.

5. In "Canción oriental" (1920) Lorca had written:

La espiga es el pan. Es Cristo
en vida y muerte cuajado.   (p. 258)

> The spike [of wheat] is bread. It's Christ
> in life and death congealed.

6. I have been told that there are Spanish folksongs where the mule replaces the ox, but I have not been able to verify it.

After these verses the poem returns to the past tenses with which it opened. It is now time to make explicit what has already been hinted at: the lost son is the poet at an earlier time in his life when he believed that Christ's sacrifice was redemptive, that His death on the Cross was in fact a victory over death. To put it more simply, the lost son is lost faith. By saying that his son was a giant, he stresses the strength of his former faith, but, alas, the dead are stronger than his son and they are able to consume pieces of heaven (reduce hope). If his son had been a bear, that is, a wild animal unaware of the promise implicit in Christ's death, he would not fear the stealth of vicious and evil beings (alligators)dragons), nor would he have seen the sea (death) degraded and wounded by the throng of the regiments (another allusion to World War I seen as an example of unbridled evil and death).

At this point the poet turns again to the future tense, saying he will wrap himself on the hard canvas so as not to feel the cold of the mosses of death.[7] The cold that he would guard himself against is the same cold that surrounds the chalice. It is not easy to imagine the meaning of the next verse: "I know very well that they will give me a sleeve or the necktie." It may be an allusion to preparations for a funeral. Whatever the verse may mean, the final verses are joined to it by the adversative conjunction *pero* (but), which tends to cancel the suggestion of the obscure verse. The poet then announces that in the center of the mass he will break the rudder, that is, he will no longer accept direction or guidance from the ship symbolic of the Church of Christ;[8] and there will come to the stone the madness of penguins and gulls who will make those who sleep and those who sing on the street corners say that he had a son who was his alone, because he was his son.

In the folklore of many times and places birds have symbolized, among other things, spirits and human souls. Gulls and penguins are at first glance an odd pair to express such symbolic values: the first are strong fliers, the second are earth-bound; but they both do have an important common characteristic: both are intimately associated with the sea, which so often symbolizes death. The word *piedra* (stone) is not much used in the early poetry of Lorca. In *Poeta en Nueva York*, it is used only twice (pp. 475, 481) prior to its appearance in "Iglesia abandonada," so up to this point there is not much

---

7. Martínez Nadal calls attention to the relations of *musgo* with death in *El público*, pp. 120–21.

8. Philip Cummings has told how often and how vehemently Lorca expressed to him his rejection of the Catholic Church because of its curtailment of freedom of expression and conduct. See *Songs*, pp. 177–79.

to help interpret it. But it soon acquires ominous connotations and in "Llanto por Ignacio Sánchez Mejías" its association with death is undeniable. If it has the same value in the poem we are studying, then even the *locura* (one of whose meanings is "spiritual exaltation") of the birds will come down to the stony fact of death and make the living and the dead proclaim that his son (the one who once believed that Christ's mortal sacrifice for love was a victory over death) was his alone, that is, born of his hope and belief rather than sent by God.

Despite the seemingly bizarre elements contained in "Iglesia abandonada," elements whose correct interpretation must for now remain problematical, it is hardly possible to doubt that it expresses the poet's loss of faith in the efficacy of Christ's mission and that this loss of faith contributes powerfully to the air of desolation that pervades the world of *Poeta en Nueva York*.

For Lorca Christ was the supreme example of sacrificial love. Some of his poetic allusions to Christ's sacrifice for love are relatively open; others are less so. In the poem titled "Crucifixión" the amount of appropriate Biblical material it contains assures us that it is a modern reworking of the Biblical story. Early in the poem we read that the blood that descended the mountain found no chalices to contain it; at the end of the poem that same unreceived blood was following the Pharisees with the bleating of a lamb ("*mientras la sangre los seguía con un balido de cordero,*" p. 533), which suggests that the sacrificed blood of the Saviour remains ineffective. When in chapter 5 I analyzed the poem called "Ruina," I noted that on the approach of death the besieged poet tossed them a bleating lamb and I suggested that this was a clear allusion to the Paschal Lamb.

In Spanish the cry of the lamb is correctly expressed by the verb *balar*. Now it is a curious and little-noticed fact that twice in *Poeta en Nueva York* Lorca uses the verb *balar* to express the voice of the cow.[9] Both occur in the poem called "Vaca," whose last stanza reads as follows:

Que ya se fue balando
por el derribo de los cielos yertos
donde meriendan muerte los borrachos.   (p. 504)

> (That) she has gone off bleating
> through the ruin of rigid skies
> where the drunkards lunch on death.

9. C. Marcilly has pointed out the significant relationship between *balar* and *vaca*. See his "Notes pour l'Étude de la Pensée Religieuse de F. García Lorca: Crucifixión," p. 518.

The allusive power of *balar*, derived from its association with the sacrificed Lamb of God, is transferred to the cow and to other things as well. In an earlier poem called "Burla de don Pedro a caballo" it became the secret voice of the afternoon bleating in the sky (*"Voz secreta de tarde / balaba por el cielo,"* p. 463). In a later poem titled "Tierra y luna" it is the naked earth that bleats in the sky (*"Es la tierra desnuda que bala por el cielo,"* p. 645). But whether applied to the cow or something else, it reminds us of an enduring sorrow whose origins lead back to Golgotha.

If the poet came to believe that Christ died in vain and that God has withdrawn his Grace from the world, then it is easy to understand his own "heaven-willed death" and his insistence on the finality of death. In "Panorama ciego de Nueva York" we may read that women who die in childbirth know of that finality:

Y las que mueren de parto saben en la última hora
que todo rumor es piedra y toda huella latido.   (p. 495)

> And those who die in childbirth know at the final hour
> that every murmur is stone and every footprint a heartbeat.

In "Cementerio judío," it is suggested that corpses sense that after death there is only more death:

Cuando los cadáveres sienten en los pies
la terrible claridad de otra luna enterrada.   (p. 518)

> When the corpses feel in their feet
> the terrible clarity of another buried moon.

Even in "Vals en las ramas," death is triumphant:

Llegará un torso de sombra
coronado de laurel.   (p. 529)

> A torso of shadow will arrive
> with laurel crowned.

Death being final in the sense already suggested, it is not surprising that the poet applies to *cielo* (sky-heaven) such adjectives as *vacío* (empty), *hueco* (hollow), *solo* (alone), and *desierto* (deserted). Some of the forlorn air of Lorca's New York is conveyed by the way he presents its physical appearance:

Desfiladeros de cal aprisionaban un cielo vacío
donde sonaban las voces de los que mueren bajo el guano.   (p. 485)

> Canyons of lime imprisoned an empty sky
> where sounded the shouts of those who die under the guano.

"Navidad en el Hudson," which one might expect to bring some of the hope of the Nativity, insists rather on *"El mundo solo por el cielo solo"* ("The lonely world in the lonely sky," p. 491). At least twice in *Poeta en Nueva York*, *cielo* is associated with some kind of cosmic death. Here is one example:

Cielos yertos en declive, donde las colonias de planetas
rueden por las playas con los objetos abandonados.   (p. 480)

> Rigid sloping skies, where the colonies of planets
> will roll along the beaches with abandoned things.

We have seen *yerto* before, but it may still be worth mentioning that it has a long history of association with death because of its primary meaning and because it is so frequently used in the phrase *yerto de frío* (stiff with cold).

So the sky is empty and beyond it there is nothing. In "La aurora" early-rising New Yorkers sense this to be so:

Los primeros que salen comprenden con sus huesos
que no habrá paraíso ni amores deshojados.   (p. 497)

> The first to go out understand with their bones
> that there will be neither heaven nor loves fulfilled.

In "Nocturno del hueco" the poet concludes in his own first person: *"No hay siglo nuevo ni luz reciente"* ("There is no new century or recent light," p. 509). "Light" probably stands for Christ ("I am the light of the world"), but if he died to no avail, his light is no more. In the "Oda a Walt Whitman" the poet advises Walt: *"Duerme, no queda nada"* ("Sleep, nothing remains," p. 526).

Something does remain: the Earth with its constant renewal of life:

Aquí solo existe la Tierra.
La tierra con sus puertas de siempre
que llevan al rubor de los frutos.   (p. 496)

Here only the Earth exists.
The earth with its gates of forever
that lead to the flush of the fruits.

In "Grito hacia Roma," where Lorca depicts the Church as ineffectual in a world of violence and injustice, it is important to note that he does not call out for Heaven's will to be done but only for Earth's will to be done:

porque queremos que se cumpla la voluntad de la Tierra
que da sus frutos para todos.   (p. 522)

because we want Earth's will to be done,
Earth which bears its fruits for all.

The final stanza of a poem Lorca wrote in 1919 runs like this:

. . . Y el hombre miserable
es un ángel caído.
La tierra es el probable
Paraíso perdido.   (p. 277)

. . . And wretched man
is a fallen angel.
The earth is the probable
Paradise lost.

As we have seen in the preceding paragraph, in Poeta en Nueva York Lorca still proclaims that there will be no heaven. What hope man may venture to entertain must be found on this abiding earth; the poet wishes the generous will of earth to be realized, but it is only a wish.

7

Conclusions

Almost any generalization that might be advanced as one of the conclusions of a study of *Poeta en Nueva York* has already been recorded somewhere in the now-considerable body of critical writing about that book. One of the first and most obvious generalizations inspired by the book is that it is an indictment of New York or of modern civilization as represented by New York. From the earliest reviews of *Poeta en Nueva York* to the latest essays about it, one continues to find some version of this view. Let us sample three versions of it.

In 1940 Conrad Aiken, reviewing the book for the *New Republic*, wrote these words: "There has been no more terribly acute critic of America than this steel-conscious and death-conscious Spaniard with his curious passion for the modernities of nickel and tinfoil and nitre, and for the eternities of the desert and the moon. He hated us, and rightly, for the right reasons."[1] Seventeen years later Gustavo Correa expressed the following judgment: "The poet,

1. *New Republic* 103 (2 Sept. 1940): 309.

having been transplanted to an environment dominated almost exclusively by a mechanical civilization, suddenly finds himself deprived of his spontaneous and natural communication with the affirmative world of cosmic nature, and his inner world suffers a collapse that produces a temporary crumbling of all his values. This is without doubt the meaning of this book."[2] Twenty years later still Allen Josephs had this to say: "If we can see *Poeta en Nueva York* convincingly as a deliberately apocalyptic vision of Anglo-Saxon America, as a vatic rejection of the myopia of materialism and the anthropocentrism or even solipcism of modern industrialized society, then we can begin to see that the poet's responses to the city are in fact traditionally Spanish, reactionary, perhaps nearly evangelistic: the poet is a voice crying, sometimes screaming, in an urban wilderness."[3] All of these versions and many similar ones are in a general way warranted, but questions of nuance and proportion and perspective may stir in the reader's mind some uneasiness about them.

Uninformed as he was about America, could Lorca rightly be considered an acute critic of America? And how much of America does the *us* he is alleged to hate encompass? Professor Josephs shows himself completely aware that what he calls Lorca's "denunciatory vision of industrial society" occupies only about a third of the New York poems and yet he assigns to them the larger purpose of the book. How do we know they express the larger purpose? And if the denunciation is of Anglo-Saxon America only, why in "Grito hacia Roma" are disasters to be visited on Rome as well as on New York? As for Professor Correa's interpretation of the meaning of the book, does it really represent the temporary crumbling of all of Lorca's values or does it rather represent a reelaboration and more insistent affirmation of some of them?

Taken together, the respectable opinions I have quoted and the possibly captious questions I have asked illustrate for me the present state of the accumulated criticism of *Poeta en Nueva York*. Much of what has been written about it strikes me as true in some sense or to some degree or in some perspective, but no one study puts enough of these partial truths together to give an accurate picture of any aspect of the whole. I make no claim to full success in this regard, but I believe that I can draw a few conclusions that will hit the target closer to its center.

Some critics have tried to read *Poeta en Nueva York* as a modern reworking of an ancient myth. So far they have failed. The book does not exhibit the kind

2. *La poesía mítica de Federico García Lorca* (Eugene, Ore.: University of Oregon Press, 1957), p. 114.

3. "Lorca's Anglo-Saxon Apocalypse," *García Lorca Review* 4 (Spring 1976): 85.

of unity that might have resulted from the retelling of a well-known myth, which is not to say that its mythic content is nil. But the book does have a kind of psychic unity, because it is the expression not so much of discrete themes as of a total experience, that of Lorca in America. As is evident in chapter 3, the different sections of the book reveal some variety of setting and separate theme; but more impressive is the fact that the themes that arise out of the poet's private preoccupations lurk in the depths of nearly all of the poems ostensibly about what he called "the poetic world of New York" while echoes and glimmers of New York infiltrate his own poetic world, whether experienced in New York or in Vermont. The unity and expressive energy of the book were generated by the fusion of two sets of passions: those that flared up from his reaction to a seemingly ominous and alien city and those that issued from the inner turmoil he brought to New York from his native Spain. He knew what he was doing when he called his book *Poeta en Nueva York*. The title captures both the dual nature of what he wanted to express and the subordination of the city to the poet.

Among the major themes treated in *Poeta en Nueva York*, three assume special importance in the book and in the subsequent history of the author's artistic production. They are social injustice, dark love, and loss of religious faith. All had appeared to a limited degree before the writing of the New York poems, but in these poems they appear more fully elaborated and with greater insistence. The first of the three is the most obvious and requires the least comment.

If Lorca had been a well-informed economist or sociologist—and we may rejoice that he was not—he would have known that the injustice and suffering he saw in New York could have been matched in many communities in many parts of the world, including, for example, the Asturian miners and the Andalusian farm workers of his own country. If he reacted violently to the American metropolis, it was perhaps for four major reasons: New York wore for him an alien face; whatever New York represented for him was represented on a scale too large to be ignored; New York was floundering in the depths of the Great Depression; and Lorca came to New York predisposed to social protest, since one of the elements of his personal crisis was a feeling of social constraint. In chapter 4 I tried to describe not only that part of *Poeta en Nueva York* that deals with denunciation and protest but also the poet's enduring concern with these matters after his return to Spain. And it is not unreasonable to surmise that the social conscience aroused and fortified in New York played a major part in his increasing devotion to writing for the theater, which, as he once said, allows a more direct contact with the masses (p. 1771).

In a 1934 interview Lorca expressed the desire "to take to the theater themes and problems that people are afraid to approach" (p. 1767). As we shall shortly note, he realized this desire in at least one play. The particular theme of interest here is that of dark love. In chapter 5, I showed that it was related to social constraints, to death, and even, indirectly, to loss of faith in eternal life. Now what I wish to suggest is that in *Poeta en Nueva York* it blossomed into a major theme that would persist throughout the remainder of Lorca's literary career.

Dark love is introduced early but cautiously, which is to say, ambiguously. It is probably present in "Fábula y rueda de los tres amigos"; it is certainly present in "Tu infancia en Menton," both poems belonging to the very first section of the book; it slips unobtrusively in and out of several poems in the section called "Calles y sueños"; it is more apparent in "Poemas del lago Edem Mills"; it is more or less hidden in "El niño Stanton" and some of the poems of "Introducción a la muerte"; it is alluded to in "Grito hacia Roma"; it receives its fullest and most explicit treatment in "Oda a Walt Whitman"; and it is alluded to once more in "Pequeño vals vienés." I mention all of these titles merely as a way of illustrating how large the theme bulks in *Poeta en Nueva York*. Only the initiated would detect the theme in many of the poems listed, which probably means that Lorca was still chary of bringing the theme openly into his writing. But under the aegis of the noble poet Walt Whitman, he ventures to introduce and defend homosexual love in a way that most readers could not miss. It was not an important theme before the writing of the New York poems; afterward it was. It is thought to be the major theme of the lost collection titled *Sonetos del amor oscuro*; it is important in the poems collected under the title *Diván del Tamarit* (1936); it is present in the play *Así que pasen cinco años* (1931); and it is the central theme of the posthumously published play called *El público*, a work which represents the full realization of Lorca's expressed desire to take to the theater themes and problems that most writers were afraid to tackle.

The religious theme is treated more fully and more despairingly in *Poeta en Nueva York* than in any other of Lorca's works. Its leitmotif might well be "the lonely world in the lonely sky." What world and sky are lonesome for is God. It is not that God doesn't exist or is dead. God, having sacrificed his only Son to no avail, has withdrawn His Grace and is no longer accessible to man. That is the meaning of the application to sky (heaven) of such adjectives as "empty" and "deserted." That is what adds greater poignancy to Lorca's dark forebodings about death. And it even associates itself in one way or another with the torment of love. That this is so can be illustrated with a number of verses from the most extensive poem on inverted love, "Oda a Walt Whitman." The following verses have already been quoted, but we need to look at them once more.

Puede el hombre, si quiere, conducir su deseo
por vena de coral o celeste desnudo.
Mañana los amores serán rocas y el Tiempo
una brisa que viene dormida por las ramas.   (p. 525)

> Man may, if he wishes, conduct his desire
> by vein of coral pink or sky-blue nude.
> Tomorrow love affairs will be rocks and Time
> a breeze that comes through the branches asleep.

Man has a certain freedom to choose his style of love, but he must know that it will last only until the morrow. The brevity of love is punctuated by the imminence and rock-like finality of death. Another stanza of the same poem begins with the despairing notion that the world is agony, agony, agony, and ends with the verse: *"y la vida no es noble, ni buena, ni sagrada"* ("and life is not noble or good or sacred"), p. 525. How can life be sacred in a world abandoned by God?

The themes of social injustice, dark love, and lost faith, under the never-failing shadow of death, are the streams that converge and commingle in Lorca's American experience to imbue the powerful verses of *Poeta en Nueva York* with their unmistakable flavor of desolation and mortal anguish.

Bibliography of works cited

Aiken, Conrad. "Sobre García Lorca: *The Poet in New York* and Other Poems."
   New Republic 103 (2 Sept. 1940): 309.

Alonso, Dámaso. *Poetas españoles contemporáneos*. Madrid: Editorial Gredos, 1952.

Auclair, Marcelle. *Enfances et mort de García Lorca*. Paris: Editions du Seuil,
   1968.

Craige, Betty Jean. *Lorca's Poet in New York*. Lexington: The University of
   Kentucky Press, 1977.

Dalí, Salvador. *The Secret Life of Salvador Dalí*. New York: Dial Press, 1942.

Eisenberg, Daniel. *Poeta en Nueva York: Historia y problemas de un texto de
   Lorca*. Barcelona: Editorial Ariel, 1976.

Ferguson, George. *Signs and Symbols in Christian Art*. New York: Oxford University Press, 1966.

Friedrich, Hugo. *Estructura de la lírica moderna*. Barcelona: Seix Barral, 1974.

Fusero, Clemente. *García Lorca*. Milano: Dall 'Oglio, 1969.

García Lorca, Federico. *Impresiones y paisajes*. Granada: Tipografía P. V. Traveset,
   1918.

————. *Poeta en Nueva York*. Mexico: Editorial Seneca, 1940.

————. *The Poet in New York and Other Poems of Federico* García Lorca. Translated by Rolphe Humphries. New York: W. W. Norton & Co., 1940.

————. *Poet in New York*. Translated by Ben Belitt. New York: Grove Press, 1955.

————. *Three Tragedies of Federico García Lorca*. Translated by Richard L. O'Connell and James Graham-Luján. Introduction by the Poet's Brother Francisco. New York: New Directions, 1947.

————. *Obras completas*. 11th ed. Madrid: Aguilar, 1966.

————. *Autógrafos I*. Edited by Rafael Martínez Nadal. Oxford: The Dolphin Book Co., 1975.

————. *Autógrafos II: El público*. Edited by Rafael Martínez Nadal. Oxford: The Dolphin Book Co., 1976.

————. *Songs*. Translated by Philip Cummings. Edited by Daniel Eisenberg. Pittsburgh: Duquesne University Press, 1976.

Josephs, Allen. "Lorca's Anglo-Saxon Apocalypse." *García Lorca Review* 4 (Spring 1976): 75–90.

Kandinsky, Wassily. *Concerning the Spiritual in Art*. Translated by Francis Golffing, Michael Harrison, and Ferdinand Osterlag. New York: Wittenborn, Schultz, Inc., 1947.

Laffranque, Marie. *Les Idées Esthétiques de Federico García Lorca*. Paris: Centre de Recherches Hispaniques, 1967.

Larrea, Juan. "Asesinado por el ciclo," *España Peregrina* 1 (1940): 251–56.

Marcilly, C. "Notes pour l'Étude de la Pensée Religieuse de F. García Lorca: Crucifixión." *Bulletin Hispanique* 64 bis (1962): 507–25.

————. *Ronde et Fable de la Solitude à New York*. Paris: Ediciones Hispano-Americanas, 1962.

Martín, Eutimio. "¿Existe una versión definitiva de *Poeta en Nueva York*?" *Insula* 310 (Sept. 1972): 1, 10.

Martínez Nadal, Rafael. *El público: Amor, teatro y caballos en la obra de Federico García Lorca*. Oxford: The Dolphin Book Co., 1970.

Poggioli, Renato. *The Theory of the Avant-Garde*. New York: Harper & Row, 1971.

Pollin, Alice M. *A Concordance to the Plays and Poems of Federico García Lorca*. Ithaca, N.Y.: Cornell University Press, 1975.

Ramos-Gil, Carlos. *Claves líricas de García Lorca*. Madrid: Aguilar, 1967.

Read, Herbert. *A Concise History of Modern Painting*. New York: Praeger, 1968.

Río, Ángel del. *Estudios sobre literatura contemporánea española*. Madrid: Editorial Gredos, 1966.

Rivas Cherif, Cipriano. "La muerte y la pasión de Federico García Lorca." *Excelsior* (Mexico), 6, 13, 27 Jan. 1957.

Saez, Richard. "The Ritual Sacrifice in Lorca's *Poet in New York*." In *Lorca: A*

Collection of Critical Essays. Edited by Manuel Durán. Englewood Cliffs, N.Y.: Prentice Hall, 1962. Pp. 108–29.

Schonberg, Jean-Louis. *Federico García Lorca: El hombre, la obra.* Mexico: Compañia general de ediciones, 1959.

————. *À la Recherche de Lorca.* Neuchâtel: la Baconnière, 1966.

Schwartz, Kessel. "García Lorca en Vermont." *Hispania* 42 (1959): 50–55.

Semprun Donahue, Moraima. "Cristo en Lorca." *Explicación de textos literarios* 4 (1975–76): 23–34.

Index